Tech Interviews Demystified

Cracking Coding and System Design Questions Ace your next tech job interview with confidence

THOMPSON CARTER

Table of Content

TABLE OF CONTENTS

Introduction

Tech Interviews Demystified: Cracking Coding and System Design Questions

The landscape of technical interviews has evolved significantly in recent years, with companies placing a strong emphasis on assessing not only technical expertise but also problem-solving abilities, communication skills, and cultural fit. As the tech industry continues to grow, more and more candidates are competing for positions at leading companies, and the interview process has become increasingly competitive. **"Tech Interviews Demystified: Cracking Coding and System Design Questions"** is designed to help you navigate this challenging process and provide you with the tools, strategies, and confidence you need to succeed in coding and system design interviews.

This book is not just another guide to the theoretical aspects of coding interviews; it is a comprehensive resource designed to help you tackle both the technical and non-technical components of the interview. It provides practical, hands-on strategies for solving common coding problems, designing scalable systems, and effectively communicating your thought process. The goal is to help you become a well-rounded candidate who excels in both problem-solving and the interpersonal aspects of interviews.

Who is This Book For?

This book is ideal for anyone preparing for tech interviews, whether you are a **fresh graduate** just entering the job market, an **experienced developer** looking to switch companies, or someone hoping to land a **position at a top tech company** like Google, Facebook, or Amazon. The content is designed to be accessible to both beginners and seasoned professionals, providing foundational knowledge for newcomers while offering in-depth insights for experienced candidates looking to refine their skills.

What Will You Learn?

Throughout the book, we will cover the key areas necessary for acing technical interviews:

1. **Coding Interviews:**
   o How to solve a wide variety of problems across different domains, including **arrays, strings, trees, graphs**, and **dynamic programming**.

- o Techniques for breaking down complex problems into manageable steps, optimizing solutions for time and space complexity, and handling edge cases.

- o The importance of **clear communication** during coding interviews, including how to explain your thought process, identify possible improvements, and troubleshoot during debugging.

2. **System Design Interviews:**

- o The principles behind designing scalable, efficient, and maintainable systems in real-world contexts. You will learn how to approach problems like **designing a URL shortener, building a social media platform**, or **creating a distributed file system**.

- o How to break down system design problems, address non-functional requirements such as **scalability, availability**, and **fault tolerance**, and communicate your design choices effectively.

- o A step-by-step approach for tackling these interviews, from understanding requirements and defining components to optimizing performance and refining your solution.

3. **Behavioral Interviews:**

   o Tips for preparing for behavioral questions that assess your soft skills, including **leadership**, **problem-solving**, **communication**, and **teamwork**.

   o How to answer questions using the **STAR method** (Situation, Task, Action, Result), with examples that highlight how to present yourself as a valuable asset to the team.

4. **Mock Interviews and Practice:**

   o The importance of practicing under realistic conditions through **mock interviews**. We provide actionable tips for simulating real interview scenarios, managing your time, staying calm under pressure, and receiving valuable feedback to improve.

   o How to approach practice strategically to ensure you're consistently improving and building confidence before your actual interviews.

5. **Interview Etiquette and Communication Skills:**

o Best practices for presenting yourself professionally, including non-verbal communication, maintaining a positive attitude, and handling nerves.

o How to communicate effectively with interviewers, ensuring that your answers are clear, concise, and well-organized.

How This Book Is Structured

The book is structured to guide you through every stage of the tech interview process. We start with the foundational elements of coding interviews, gradually progressing to more complex system design topics, followed by preparation strategies for behavioral interviews. The final chapters focus on **mock interviews, feedback**, and **how to make the best impression** during the interview process.

- **Chapter 1** through **Chapter 12** focus on coding problems, covering common interview topics, including arrays, strings, linked lists, trees, and more.
- **Chapter 13** through **Chapter 19** dive into system design concepts, guiding you through scalable architectures, databases, caching, load balancing, and real-world examples.

- **Chapter 20** through **Chapter 23** focus on behavioral questions, mock interviews, and communication skills.

- **Chapter 24** and **Chapter 25** offer final tips for performing well under pressure and ensuring you make the best impression during the interview.

Why This Book Is Different

While many coding interview books focus solely on algorithms and data structures, **"Tech Interviews Demystified"** offers a comprehensive, balanced approach. It not only teaches you how to solve problems but also provides practical strategies for navigating the entire interview process. You'll learn how to think critically, communicate effectively, and stay confident under pressure—skills that are just as crucial as technical knowledge.

Continuous Learning and Improvement

This book is just the beginning of your preparation journey. **Tech interviews** are dynamic and constantly evolving. To keep your skills sharp, we include recommendations for **additional resources** such as online coding platforms, system design books, and interview prep websites. Whether you need help refining your coding skills or improving your system design knowledge, we provide the resources that will allow you to continue learning and improving even after you've finished reading the book.

In Conclusion

Success in **tech interviews** requires more than just technical knowledge—it's about how you approach problems, communicate your solutions, and demonstrate your ability to thrive in high-pressure environments. **"Tech Interviews Demystified"** is designed to give you the edge you need to succeed in the competitive world of technical interviews. With a blend of in-depth technical content, practical interview strategies, and expert insights, this book will help you build the confidence and skills necessary to ace any coding or system design interview.

CHAPTER 1

INTRODUCTION TO TECH INTERVIEWS

Tech interviews are often seen as one of the most challenging aspects of the job application process, especially in fields such as software engineering, data science, and product management. However, understanding what to expect and how to approach each stage can help you navigate the process with confidence. In this chapter, we'll introduce you to the tech interview process, break down the various stages, and provide strategies for preparing mentally and physically for success.

What to Expect in a Tech Interview

Tech interviews are designed to assess your technical knowledge, problem-solving abilities, and overall fit for the company. The interview process typically involves a combination of **coding tests**, **system design questions**, and **behavioral interviews**, with each stage evaluating a different set of skills.

While the specific structure of the interview can vary between companies, you can expect the following:

- **Problem-solving skills:** Expect coding challenges that test your ability to think critically and write efficient code.

- **Knowledge of algorithms and data structures:** You'll need to demonstrate a deep understanding of commonly used algorithms and data structures (e.g., arrays, linked lists, trees, graphs, hash maps, etc.).

- **System design:** For more senior roles, system design questions may evaluate your ability to architect scalable, efficient, and reliable systems.

- **Behavioral questions:** These questions assess your interpersonal skills, teamwork, and cultural fit within the company.

- **Communication skills:** Interviewers will evaluate how effectively you can explain your thought process, solve problems collaboratively, and communicate technical concepts.

The key to excelling in tech interviews lies in preparing for all of these aspects—coding, system design, and behavioral—and presenting yourself as a well-rounded candidate.

The Different Stages of the Interview Process

Tech interviews usually consist of multiple stages, each with its own focus. Here's a breakdown of the most common stages:

1. Screening (Phone/Video Interview): The first stage is often a **screening interview**, typically conducted over the phone or via video conference. The primary goal of this stage is to assess your basic technical abilities and determine if you're a good fit for the role. You might be asked to solve coding problems on a whiteboard or a shared code editor (e.g., **CoderPad**, **Google Docs**). The interviewer will also ask about your previous experience and your interest in the company.

- **What to expect:** Coding problems involving algorithms and data structures, a brief discussion about your background and experience, and questions to assess your problem-solving approach.
- **Tip:** Prepare by practicing coding problems and reviewing your resume. Focus on explaining your thought process clearly.

16

2. Technical Interview (Coding Challenges): In this stage, you'll face a series of coding problems that test your ability to solve problems efficiently. You may be asked to solve problems on a whiteboard, in an online code editor, or even via a collaborative tool. The interviewer will assess both the correctness of your solution and your approach to problem-solving.

- **What to expect:** You will be given coding problems involving common algorithms and data structures. The problems will range from easy to hard, and you'll be expected to write clean, efficient code. Often, you will need to explain your approach, analyze the time complexity of your solution (Big O notation), and optimize your code.
- **Tip:** Practice solving coding problems on platforms like **LeetCode**, **HackerRank**, and **CodeSignal**. Focus on writing optimal code and communicating your thought process as you work through the problem.

3. Behavioral Interview (Soft Skills Evaluation): The behavioral interview focuses on assessing your interpersonal skills, cultural fit, and how well you align with the company's values. In this stage, you'll be asked questions that evaluate your previous experiences, decision-making, conflict resolution, teamwork, and leadership skills.

- **What to expect:** Common behavioral interview questions include:
    - "Tell me about a time you faced a challenge at work and how you overcame it."
    - "How do you handle conflicts with team members?"
    - "Describe a time when you showed leadership."
- **Tip:** Use the **STAR method** (Situation, Task, Action, Result) to structure your answers. Be specific about your role and contributions to past projects, and emphasize how you've demonstrated problem-solving and collaboration.

4. Final Interview (Onsite or Virtual): The final interview stage often involves a more in-depth assessment and a mix of technical and behavioral evaluations. Some companies may invite you to an **onsite interview**, while others may conduct this stage virtually. Expect to solve coding challenges, participate in system design discussions, and engage in behavioral interviews.

- **What to expect:** A combination of coding problems, system design challenges, and behavioral questions. Some companies also test your ability to work in a collaborative setting, possibly by including a **pair programming** session or a group discussion.

- **Tip:** Prepare for a rigorous day by practicing system design problems and reviewing complex coding questions. Make sure to get a good night's sleep before the interview day and come prepared to explain your solutions clearly.

Understanding Coding and System Design Questions

1. Coding Questions: Coding questions are typically the bread and butter of tech interviews. These questions test your ability to write clean, efficient, and correct code under time pressure. Common coding problems include:

- **Sorting algorithms** (e.g., merge sort, quick sort).
- **Searching algorithms** (e.g., binary search).
- **Graph and tree traversal** (e.g., breadth-first search, depth-first search).
- **Dynamic programming** (e.g., Fibonacci series, longest common subsequence).

- **String manipulation** (e.g., palindrome checking, substring search).

- **Tip:** Focus on mastering common data structures (arrays, linked lists, trees, etc.) and algorithms. Practice solving problems within a set time frame to simulate real interview conditions. Pay attention to time and space complexity (Big O analysis) to optimize your solutions.

2. System Design Questions: System design questions are more common in senior-level interviews but may appear at junior levels for companies that value scalable architectures. These questions assess your ability to design systems that are efficient, scalable, and reliable. You may be asked to design anything from a simple web application to a complex distributed system.

- **What to expect:** You will be asked to design a system by considering factors such as data storage, data flow, scaling, redundancy, load balancing, and fault tolerance. You'll need to consider how to handle large volumes of data, ensure reliability, and provide a user-friendly experience.

- **Tip:** Focus on the fundamentals of **scalability**, **load balancing**, **caching**, **databases** (SQL vs. NoSQL), and **microservices**. Be prepared to explain your design decisions clearly and justify trade-offs.

How to Prepare Mentally and Physically for Interviews

1. Mental Preparation: A tech interview can be mentally taxing, especially when you're solving complex coding problems or explaining your system design. Mental preparation is key to staying calm, focused, and confident during the interview.

- **Focus on problem-solving**: View each question as an opportunity to showcase your problem-solving skills. Break down the problem step by step, and don't rush into coding immediately. It's essential to first understand the problem fully, discuss your approach with the interviewer, and then proceed with coding.

- **Practice stress management**: Interviews can feel high-stakes, but practicing deep breathing exercises and maintaining a positive mindset can help calm nerves. Remember, the interview is an opportunity to learn and grow, not just to impress.

- **Visualize success**: Positive visualization techniques can help build confidence. Picture yourself solving

21

the problems successfully and handling tough questions with poise. This mental rehearsal can reduce anxiety and boost your performance.

2. Physical Preparation: Physical well-being is often overlooked in interview preparation, but it can play a significant role in your performance. Sleep, nutrition, and exercise can all affect your ability to think clearly and stay focused during your interview.

- **Sleep well**: Aim for 7–8 hours of restful sleep before the interview. A well-rested mind is more alert and sharp, allowing you to think clearly and solve problems effectively.
- **Stay hydrated and eat well**: Make sure you are hydrated and have a balanced meal before your interview. Avoid caffeine overload, as it can cause anxiety and jitters. Choose a healthy meal with complex carbohydrates and proteins to fuel your brain.
- **Exercise regularly**: Physical exercise helps reduce stress and improve concentration. Incorporating short walks or light workouts before the interview can help you stay relaxed and maintain mental clarity.

In conclusion, **Tech Interviews** can seem daunting, but with the right preparation, mindset, and approach, you can succeed with confidence. By understanding the different stages of the interview, preparing for both technical and behavioral questions, and taking care of your mental and physical health, you will be ready to tackle any interview challenge. In the next chapters, we will dive deeper into coding problems, system design techniques, and interview strategies to ensure that you are fully equipped for success.

CHAPTER 2

THE CODING INTERVIEW -
WHAT TO EXPECT

The coding interview is one of the most important and challenging parts of the hiring process for tech roles. It tests not only your technical skills but also your ability to think logically, communicate clearly, and solve problems efficiently. Understanding what to expect in a coding interview, what interviewers look for, and how to prepare will give you the edge you need to succeed. This chapter will guide you through these essential aspects.

Overview of the Coding Interview

The coding interview is typically the first major hurdle in the tech job application process. In this stage, you will be tasked with solving one or more coding problems that evaluate your ability to write correct, efficient, and maintainable code. These problems usually involve algorithms, data structures, and basic problem-solving skills, and may be conducted in various formats, including:

- **Whiteboard coding:** This is traditional in onsite interviews, where you'll write your solution on a whiteboard (or on paper in some cases). This is a good opportunity to show your logical thinking and coding approach, even if you're not actually typing out the code.

- **Online coding platforms:** In virtual interviews, coding challenges are often conducted using online platforms like **CoderPad**, **HackerRank**, or **LeetCode**. You'll typically code in an integrated environment that allows for real-time feedback and testing of your code.

- **Pair programming:** Some companies use pair programming in coding interviews, where you'll work with the interviewer to solve a problem collaboratively. This method allows interviewers to assess your communication skills and how well you work with others.

Regardless of the format, the goals of the interview remain the same: interviewers want to see how you approach problems, how you think through solutions, and whether you can write clean, efficient code under pressure.

What Interviewers Look for When Assessing Coding Skills

When interviewers assess your coding skills, they focus on several key attributes that indicate whether you would be a valuable member of their team. These include:

1. Problem-Solving Ability:

- **How well you break down complex problems into smaller, manageable parts**. Interviewers are keen to see your thought process as you approach a problem, especially how you approach complexity and how you simplify the solution.

- **Tip:** Always start by understanding the problem completely. Ask clarifying questions if necessary, and outline a plan before diving into coding. Think about edge cases and constraints early on.

2. Coding and Algorithmic Knowledge:

- **Your knowledge of algorithms and data structures**. This is at the heart of most coding interviews. You need to be comfortable with common data structures (arrays, linked lists, trees, etc.) and algorithms (sorting, searching, recursion, dynamic programming, etc.).

26

- **Tip:** Regularly practice coding problems on platforms like **LeetCode**, **HackerRank**, or **Codeforces** to strengthen your algorithmic knowledge.

3. Code Quality and Efficiency:

- **How clean, efficient, and maintainable your code is.** This involves not just writing a working solution but writing code that is clear, concise, and well-organized.
- **Tip:** Aim for clean, readable code with proper indentation, meaningful variable names, and logical flow. Keep performance in mind and optimize your solution when possible, but don't over-engineer your code.

4. Time and Space Complexity:

- **How you analyze and optimize the time and space complexity** of your solution (Big O notation). A good solution isn't just correct; it's efficient, especially when dealing with large inputs.
- **Tip:** After coming up with your initial solution, assess its time and space complexity. Be prepared to

discuss ways to improve efficiency, particularly if your initial solution is suboptimal.

5. Communication and Collaboration:

- **How you communicate your thought process and explain your solution**. During the interview, interviewers will be closely watching how you talk through the problem, how you articulate your reasoning, and whether you ask for help or clarification when needed.
- **Tip:** Speak your thoughts aloud. Walk the interviewer through how you are approaching the problem, and explain your reasoning. Don't be afraid to admit if you're stuck; it's better to discuss your challenges than to stay silent.

Types of Coding Problems: Algorithms, Data Structures, and Problem-Solving Techniques

Coding interviews typically revolve around problems that assess your knowledge of algorithms and data structures. Understanding the types of problems you're likely to face will help you focus your preparation. Below are the main categories of problems you will encounter:

1. Algorithms: Algorithms are step-by-step procedures used to solve specific problems. These are often at the core of coding interview questions. Common types of algorithmic problems include:

- **Sorting and Searching Algorithms:** Sorting an array or list (e.g., **QuickSort, MergeSort, BubbleSort**) and searching for elements (e.g., **Binary Search**).

- **Dynamic Programming:** Solving problems by breaking them into simpler subproblems and storing solutions to subproblems to avoid redundant work (e.g., **Fibonacci sequence, Knapsack problem**).

- **Greedy Algorithms:** Making optimal choices at each step to find a globally optimal solution (e.g., **Activity selection problem, Huffman coding**).

- **Backtracking and Recursion:** Solving problems by trying all possible solutions and backtracking when a solution fails (e.g., **N-Queens problem, Sudoku solver**).

- **Tip:** For algorithmic problems, always understand the approach before you start coding. Once you have your algorithm in mind, implement it and optimize the solution as needed.

2. Data Structures: Data structures are ways to store and organize data in order to perform operations efficiently. Common data structures used in coding problems include:

- **Arrays and Strings:** Simple data structures used to store ordered collections of elements. Problems may involve sorting, searching, or manipulating arrays or strings.

- **Linked Lists:** A linear data structure where elements are connected by pointers. Problems might involve reversing a linked list or detecting cycles.

- **Stacks and Queues:** Abstract data types for managing collections of items in a specific order. Problems often involve using these structures for balanced parentheses or implementing a queue with two stacks.

- **Trees and Graphs:** Hierarchical structures (trees) or interconnected structures (graphs). These are important for traversal problems like **Depth-First Search (DFS)** and **Breadth-First Search (BFS)**.

- **Hash Maps:** A data structure that stores key-value pairs for fast lookups. Hash maps are often used for problems like counting elements or checking if two strings are anagrams.

- **Tip:** Master the common operations of each data structure (insertion, deletion, search, etc.) and practice applying them in different contexts. Understanding how each data structure works will help you choose the most appropriate one for solving a problem.

3. Problem-Solving Techniques: Problem-solving in coding interviews often involves a systematic approach to breaking down a problem and applying algorithms and data structures. Here are some common techniques:

- **Brute Force:** The simplest approach that might involve trying all possible solutions. Often inefficient for large inputs but useful for understanding the problem.
- **Divide and Conquer:** Dividing the problem into smaller subproblems, solving each subproblem, and then combining the results (e.g., **MergeSort**).
- **Sliding Window:** A technique used to optimize problems where you need to work with contiguous subarrays (e.g., finding the maximum sum of a subarray of fixed length).

- **Two Pointers:** Using two pointers to traverse a collection (e.g., finding pairs in a sorted array that sum up to a target).

- **Binary Search:** Efficiently finding a target in a sorted collection by repeatedly dividing the search space in half.

- **Tip:** Whenever possible, apply these techniques to optimize your solutions. For example, if you can reduce the time complexity of a brute-force solution with binary search or dynamic programming, do so.

A General Roadmap to Prepare for Coding Interviews

To succeed in coding interviews, a structured and consistent preparation plan is key. Here's a roadmap to help guide your preparation:

1. Master the Basics:

- Learn the fundamentals of **data structures** and **algorithms**. Understand the time and space complexities of common operations and algorithms.

- Practice simple problems first to build confidence and get comfortable with the interview format.

2. Practice, Practice, Practice:

- Use coding platforms like **LeetCode, HackerRank,** and **CodeSignal** to solve a wide range of problems. Start with easy problems and gradually move to medium and hard-level problems.
- Aim to solve problems from different categories (arrays, trees, dynamic programming, etc.) to build versatility in your approach.

3. Understand Time and Space Complexity:

- Be able to analyze and optimize the time and space complexity of your solutions. Understanding Big O notation is crucial to writing efficient code.
- Practice problems with varying time complexity to learn how to approach both optimal and suboptimal solutions.

4. Review Common Interview Problems:

- Make a list of the most commonly asked coding interview questions and solve them repeatedly. Focus on topics like sorting, searching, dynamic programming, and recursion.
- Familiarize yourself with **blind spots** like edge cases, off-by-one errors, and overflow issues.

5. Mock Interviews and Real-time Practice:

- Simulate real interview conditions by doing mock interviews with peers or using platforms like **Pramp** or **Interviewing.io**.
- Focus on **communication**: explaining your thought process clearly and efficiently, as this is just as important as solving the problem.

In conclusion, **coding interviews** can seem intimidating, but with the right preparation and mindset, you can excel in them. Focus on mastering data structures and algorithms, honing your problem-solving techniques, and practicing regularly to build confidence and improve your speed. This chapter sets the stage for mastering coding interviews by understanding what interviewers are looking for and how to approach coding problems effectively. With diligent preparation and continuous practice, you'll be ready to face even the most challenging coding interview questions.

CHAPTER 3

DATA STRUCTURES - THE BUILDING BLOCKS OF CODING INTERVIEWS

Data structures are essential for solving coding problems efficiently. They provide ways to organize and store data, making it easier to retrieve and manipulate it. In coding interviews, you'll be expected to use data structures effectively to write clean and optimized solutions to a variety of problems. In this chapter, we'll introduce the most commonly used data structures in coding interviews, explain how they are used, and provide real-world examples of when each data structure is appropriate.

Introduction to Data Structures: Arrays, Linked Lists, Stacks, Queues, and More

Data structures are a fundamental part of computer science, and understanding them is crucial for solving problems during coding interviews. Here are the most common data structures you'll encounter:

35

1. Arrays:

- An **array** is a collection of elements that are stored in contiguous memory locations. It is one of the most basic data structures and is widely used due to its simplicity and efficiency in accessing elements by index.
- Arrays are **fixed-size**, meaning you must know the size of the array ahead of time (for static arrays). For dynamic arrays (like **ArrayLists** in Java or **vectors** in C++), the array can grow as needed.

Operations:

- **Access:** Constant time, $O(1)O(1)O(1)$.
- **Insert/Remove:** Linear time, $O(n)O(n)O(n)$, unless inserting/removing at the end (which is $O(1)O(1)O(1)$).
- **Searching:** Linear time, $O(n)O(n)O(n)$, for unsorted arrays.

When to use:

- When you need fast access to elements using an index.

- Ideal for storing collections of data when the size is known ahead of time.
- Use when you need to process data in a fixed sequence (e.g., storing a list of numbers, characters, etc.).

2. Linked Lists:

- A **linked list** is a linear data structure where elements, called **nodes**, are stored in a sequence where each node points to the next node in the list. Unlike arrays, linked lists do not require contiguous memory locations.
- There are different types of linked lists: singly linked lists, doubly linked lists, and circular linked lists.

Operations:

- **Access:** Linear time, $O(n)O(n)O(n)$, since you need to traverse the list to find an element.
- **Insert/Remove:** Constant time, $O(1)O(1)O(1)$, if you have a reference to the node.
- **Searching:** Linear time, $O(n)O(n)O(n)$, unless the list is sorted or indexed.

When to use:

- When you need efficient insertion or deletion of elements, especially at the beginning or middle of the list.
- Use when the size of the collection is unknown or when you need dynamic resizing.
- Ideal for applications where memory allocation is unpredictable or fragmented.

3. Stacks:

- A **stack** is a linear data structure that follows the **Last In First Out (LIFO)** principle, meaning the last element added is the first one to be removed. Think of a stack of plates: you add plates to the top and remove plates from the top.

Operations:

- **Push (Insert):** O(1)O(1)O(1).
- **Pop (Remove):** O(1)O(1)O(1).
- **Peek (Access the top element):** O(1)O(1)O(1).

When to use:

- When you need to reverse a sequence of operations (e.g., **undo functionality** in text editors).

- Useful in **depth-first search (DFS)** algorithms.
- When parsing expressions (e.g., evaluating expressions in postfix notation).

4. Queues:

- A **queue** is another linear data structure that follows the **First In First Out (FIFO)** principle, meaning the first element added is the first one to be removed. Think of a queue at a bank: the first person in line is the first one to be served.

Operations:

- **Enqueue (Insert):** $O(1)O(1)O(1)$.
- **Dequeue (Remove):** $O(1)O(1)O(1)$.
- **Peek (Access the front element):** $O(1)O(1)O(1)$.

When to use:

- When you need to process tasks in the order they arrive (e.g., **breadth-first search (BFS), task scheduling**).
- Ideal for implementing **queues in operating systems,** such as print jobs or processes.

- Use for managing **waiting lines**, like tickets or requests.

5. Hash Maps (Dictionaries):

- A **hash map** (also called a **hash table** or **dictionary**) is a data structure that stores key-value pairs. The keys are unique, and values can be retrieved using their associated keys. Hash maps use a **hash function** to compute an index (or hash code) that maps to where the value is stored in memory.

Operations:

- **Access:** Average $O(1)O(1)O(1)$, assuming a good hash function and low collisions.
- **Insert:** Average $O(1)O(1)O(1)$.
- **Remove:** Average $O(1)O(1)O(1)$.

When to use:

- When you need fast lookups, insertions, or deletions using a key.
- Ideal for counting frequencies (e.g., counting word frequencies in a text).

- Use when you need to implement a cache, store unique items, or map data from one domain to another.

6. Trees:

- A **tree** is a hierarchical data structure made up of nodes connected by edges. Each tree has a root node, and each node may have children. The most common type of tree is a **binary tree**, where each node has at most two children.

Operations:

- **Traversal:** $O(n)O(n)O(n)$ for visiting all nodes (inorder, preorder, postorder).
- **Insert/Search/Remove:** Varies depending on tree type, but typically $O(\log n)O(\log n)O(\log n)$ for balanced binary search trees (e.g., AVL, Red-Black Tree).

When to use:

- When you need hierarchical representation, such as file systems or organizational charts.

- Use binary trees for fast searching, inserting, and deleting in sorted data.
- Ideal for constructing efficient **search trees** or **expression trees**.

7. Graphs:

- A **graph** is a non-linear data structure made up of nodes (vertices) and edges. Graphs can be **directed** or **undirected**, and edges may have weights (for weighted graphs). Graphs are useful for representing relationships between objects, such as social networks, web pages, or road systems.

Operations:

- **Traversal:** Depth-first search (DFS) or breadth-first search (BFS), both $O(V+E)O(V + E)O(V+E)$ where VVV is the number of vertices and EEE is the number of edges.
- **Shortest path:** Algorithms like **Dijkstra's** or **Bellman-Ford**.

When to use:

- When modeling networks (e.g., internet routing, social networks).
- Ideal for pathfinding algorithms, such as finding the shortest path between two nodes.
- Useful for solving problems in operations research, such as the **travelling salesman problem**.

How Data Structures Are Used in Coding Problems

In coding interviews, understanding how to use data structures effectively is key to solving problems. Here are some common types of problems and how data structures come into play:

- **Arrays:** Often used for problems that involve searching, sorting, or manipulating a sequence of elements, such as finding duplicates, reversing elements, or calculating sums or averages.
- **Linked Lists:** Ideal for problems where elements need to be dynamically inserted or deleted without the need for reallocation, such as reversing a linked list, detecting loops, or merging sorted lists.
- **Stacks and Queues:** Used for problems involving order of operations, such as evaluating expressions,

balancing parentheses, or simulating a queue of tasks or processes.

- **Hash Maps:** Frequently used in problems that require fast lookups, such as checking for anagrams, counting word frequencies, or finding two elements that sum to a target.

- **Trees and Graphs:** Useful for problems involving hierarchical structures, such as building and traversing tree structures, finding paths in a graph, or solving problems like the **lowest common ancestor** or **shortest path** problems.

Real-World Examples and When to Use Each Data Structure

Let's go through some real-world problems and scenarios to understand when and why each data structure would be appropriate:

1. Arrays:

- **Example:** Given a list of numbers, find the largest number and its index.
   - **Why use arrays:** Arrays allow you to easily access and manipulate elements by index, making them perfect for this type of problem.

2. Linked Lists:

- **Example:** Design a social media platform where users can post, comment, and reply, with each post having a dynamic number of comments.
  - **Why use linked lists:** Linked lists are great when the number of elements is dynamic, and you need efficient insertion or deletion of posts and comments.

3. Stacks:

- **Example:** Implement an **undo feature** in a text editor that allows users to revert to the previous state.
  - **Why use stacks:** Stacks follow a LIFO order, making them perfect for tracking changes and allowing users to revert to the previous action.

4. Queues:

- **Example:** Simulate a line at a ticket counter, where customers are served in the order they arrive.
  - **Why use queues:** Queues follow a FIFO order, which mimics the behavior of a real-life line.

5. Hash Maps:

- **Example:** Given a list of words, find the frequency of each word.
  - o **Why use hash maps:** Hash maps allow fast lookups and can efficiently store key-value pairs, where the key is the word, and the value is its frequency.

6. Trees:

- **Example:** Design a file system where files are organized hierarchically with directories and subdirectories.
  - o **Why use trees:** Trees naturally represent hierarchical data, with directories as nodes and files as leaves.

7. Graphs:

- **Example:** Find the shortest path between two locations in a city using a map.
  - o **Why use graphs:** Graphs can model the city as nodes (locations) and edges (roads), and algorithms like **Dijkstra's** can find the shortest path.

In conclusion, **data structures** are fundamental building blocks in coding interviews. Mastering them will allow you to solve problems efficiently and write optimized, maintainable code. Practice implementing and using data structures regularly to deepen your understanding and prepare for interview challenges.

CHAPTER 4

ALGORITHMS - SOLVING PROBLEMS EFFICIENTLY

In tech interviews, algorithms play a central role in evaluating your problem-solving abilities. Algorithms are sets of steps or rules that you follow to solve a particular problem. Understanding how algorithms work and how to apply them efficiently is key to succeeding in coding interviews. This chapter will introduce you to common algorithms, explain the importance of time and space complexity, and guide you on how to approach algorithmic problems during interviews.

Introduction to Algorithms: Sorting, Searching, Recursion, and Dynamic Programming

Algorithms are at the core of coding interview questions. There are different types of algorithms that you will encounter, each solving problems in unique ways. Let's look at the main categories of algorithms and their applications.

1. Sorting Algorithms: Sorting algorithms are used to rearrange a collection of items into a specific order (usually ascending or descending). Sorting is a foundational concept in computer science, and many interview questions require you to implement or understand sorting algorithms.

Common Sorting Algorithms:

- **Bubble Sort**: Simple but inefficient. Repeatedly swaps adjacent elements if they are in the wrong order.
- **Selection Sort**: Selects the smallest (or largest) element and swaps it with the current position.
- **Insertion Sort**: Builds the sorted array one item at a time by repeatedly inserting the next element into its correct position.
- **Merge Sort**: A divide-and-conquer algorithm that divides the array into two halves, recursively sorts them, and merges them.
- **Quick Sort**: Another divide-and-conquer algorithm that picks a "pivot" element and partitions the array into two sub-arrays, which are then sorted.

When to use sorting:

- Sorting is commonly required when data needs to be ordered, such as arranging student grades or organizing records by date. It also plays a vital role in solving problems like **binary search** and in algorithms that depend on ordering (e.g., **heap sort**).

2. Searching Algorithms: Searching algorithms are designed to find the position of an element in a collection. They are often used to identify whether an element exists in a dataset and return its index if found.

Common Searching Algorithms:

- **Linear Search**: Starts from the first element and checks each one until the target element is found. Time complexity: $O(n)O(n)O(n)$.
- **Binary Search**: An efficient algorithm that divides the collection in half and eliminates one half from further consideration. It works only on **sorted arrays**. Time complexity: $O(\log n)O(\log n)O(\log n)$.

When to use searching:

- Use linear search for unsorted datasets or when simplicity is key. Binary search is ideal for sorted datasets, as it significantly reduces the time complexity compared to linear search.

3. Recursion: Recursion is a technique where a function calls itself to solve a problem. It's often used for problems that can be broken down into smaller subproblems of the same type, such as traversing trees or solving problems involving divide-and-conquer approaches.

Common Recursive Problems:

- **Factorial Calculation**: Finding the factorial of a number (e.g., $5!=5\times4\times3\times2\times15! = 5 \times 4 \times 3 \times 2 \times 15!=5\times4\times3\times2\times1$).
- **Fibonacci Sequence**: Finding the nth Fibonacci number, where each number is the sum of the previous two.
- **Tree Traversal**: Traversing binary trees using recursive methods like **inorder**, **preorder**, or **postorder** traversal.

When to use recursion:

- Recursion is useful for problems involving data structures like trees or graphs, where you need to break down the problem into subproblems. It's also essential in problems that naturally fit a **divide-and-conquer** approach.

4. Dynamic Programming (DP): Dynamic programming is a technique used to solve problems by breaking them down into overlapping subproblems and solving each subproblem only once. It's particularly useful for optimization problems where a solution can be built from previously solved subproblems.

Common DP Problems:

- **Fibonacci Sequence** (Optimized with memoization): Instead of recalculating Fibonacci numbers repeatedly, store the results of previously computed Fibonacci numbers.
- **Knapsack Problem**: Given a set of items with weights and values, determine the maximum value that can be carried in a knapsack of a given capacity.
- **Longest Common Subsequence**: Finding the longest subsequence common to two sequences.

When to use dynamic programming:

- Use DP when you have problems that involve breaking down a task into subproblems, and where these subproblems overlap (i.e., the same subproblem is solved multiple times). It's highly effective for optimization problems like **coin change**, **longest path**, and **matrix chain multiplication**.

Understanding Time and Space Complexity (Big O Notation)

When solving algorithmic problems in coding interviews, you need to understand **time complexity** and **space complexity**. These metrics tell you how the algorithm performs in terms of time and memory usage relative to the input size. **Big O notation** is the standard way to express time and space complexity.

1. Time Complexity: Time complexity refers to the amount of time an algorithm takes to complete as a function of the size of the input data. The most common time complexities you will encounter in coding interviews are:

- **$O(1)O(1)O(1)$**: Constant time – The algorithm takes the same amount of time regardless of the size of the input.

- **O(log n)O(\log n)O(logn)**: Logarithmic time – Common in algorithms like binary search, where the problem space is halved at each step.

- **O(n)O(n)O(n)**: Linear time – The algorithm's runtime scales directly with the input size.

- **O(nlog n)O(n \log n)O(nlogn)**: Log-linear time – Found in efficient sorting algorithms like merge sort and quick sort.

- **O(n2)O(n^2)O(n2)**: Quadratic time – Often found in algorithms involving nested loops, such as bubble sort or selection sort.

- **O(2n)O(2^n)O(2n)**: Exponential time – This indicates an algorithm that solves a problem by exploring all possibilities. This is inefficient for large inputs.

- **O(n!)O(n!)O(n!)**: Factorial time – This is the worst time complexity and occurs in algorithms that generate all permutations, such as solving the traveling salesman problem.

Tip: Focus on optimizing your algorithms to reduce time complexity. For example, aim for **O(nlog n)O(n \log n)O(nlogn)** or **O(n)O(n)O(n)** solutions instead of **O(n2)O(n^2)O(n2)** when possible.

2. Space Complexity: Space complexity refers to the amount of memory an algorithm uses as a function of the size of the input. Just like time complexity, it's important to consider space complexity to ensure your algorithm is efficient in terms of memory usage.

- **O(1)O(1)O(1)**: Constant space – The algorithm uses a fixed amount of memory, regardless of input size.
- **O(n)O(n)O(n)**: Linear space – The algorithm's space usage scales with the input size.

Tip: Aim to minimize the space complexity of your algorithm, particularly if you are working with large datasets. Consider optimizing your algorithm by using **in-place** solutions when possible (e.g., reversing an array in place instead of creating a new array).

How to Approach Algorithmic Problems in Interviews

When you're faced with an algorithmic problem during an interview, a structured approach is key to arriving at the correct solution. Here's a step-by-step method you can follow:

1. Understand the Problem:

- **Read the problem carefully**: Make sure you understand what is being asked. If something is unclear, ask questions.
- **Identify input/output formats**: What is the input to your function? What should the output be?
- **Clarify edge cases**: Consider special cases like empty arrays, large inputs, or invalid inputs.

2. Plan Your Approach:

- **Choose an appropriate algorithm**: Based on the problem, decide which algorithm or data structure is best suited. For example, if it's a sorting problem, consider whether quicksort or mergesort is the best option.
- **Think about time and space complexity**: Evaluate the efficiency of your algorithm before writing the code. Aim to optimize both time and space complexity.

3. Write the Code:

- **Start with a simple solution**: If you're unsure about the most optimized solution, start with a brute-force approach and refine it later.

- **Write clean, readable code**: Use descriptive variable names, add comments where needed, and follow good coding practices.

4. Test Your Solution:

- **Check with example inputs**: Walk through the code using the sample inputs provided in the problem description.
- **Test edge cases**: Consider corner cases like empty arrays, large numbers, or extreme values.

5. Optimize (If Necessary):

- Once your basic solution is working, look for areas to optimize. Can you reduce the time complexity by changing your approach? Could you use a more efficient data structure?

6. Explain Your Thought Process:

- During the interview, always talk through your approach. Explain why you chose the algorithm or data structure, how you're solving the problem, and what your thought process is at each stage.

- This allows the interviewer to understand how you think and helps them assess your problem-solving ability.

Conclusion

Algorithms are the heart of coding interviews, and understanding how to apply them efficiently is key to success. In this chapter, we've covered common algorithm types, explained the importance of time and space complexity, and provided a structured approach for solving algorithmic problems. By practicing these algorithms and developing a clear, methodical approach to problem-solving, you'll be well-prepared for the coding challenges that await you in your next tech interview.

CHAPTER 5

SOLVING CODING CHALLENGES WITH ARRAYS

Arrays are one of the most fundamental data structures and are commonly used in coding interview problems. They provide a simple and efficient way to store and access data. However, knowing how to efficiently solve array-related problems and optimizing your solutions is key to excelling in coding interviews. In this chapter, we'll look at common array problems, how to optimize array-based solutions, and real-world examples of when and how to use arrays effectively.

Common Array Problems in Tech Interviews

Arrays are a versatile data structure and can be used to solve a wide variety of problems. Here are some common array-based problems you may encounter in coding interviews:

1. Finding Duplicates:

- Problem: Given an array of integers, find all the duplicate elements.

59

- Challenge: This problem can be tricky when working with large arrays, as the brute force approach (comparing each element with every other element) can lead to an inefficient solution with a time complexity of $O(n2)O(n^2)O(n2)$.

- **Optimized Approach:** Use a **hash set** or **hash map** to track the elements you've seen so far, which allows you to identify duplicates in **linear time $O(n)O(n)O(n)$**.

Example:

python

```python
def find_duplicates(arr):
    seen = set()
    duplicates = []
    for num in arr:
        if num in seen:
            duplicates.append(num)
        else:
            seen.add(num)
    return duplicates
```

2. Merging Intervals:

- Problem: Given a list of intervals, merge all overlapping intervals and return a list of non-overlapping intervals.
- Challenge: Sorting the intervals and efficiently merging them can be a bit tricky if not done in the correct order.
- **Optimized Approach:** First, sort the intervals by their start time. Then, iterate through the intervals, merging them when they overlap and adding them to the result list.

Example:

python

```python
def merge_intervals(intervals):
    if not intervals:
        return []

    intervals.sort(key=lambda x: x[0])   # Sort intervals by start time
    merged = [intervals[0]]

    for current in intervals[1:]:
        last_merged = merged[-1]
```

```
    if current[0] <= last_merged[1]:  # If overlapping
        merged[-1] = [last_merged[0], max(last_merged[1],
current[1])]  # Merge
    else:
        merged.append(current)  # No overlap, add as a new
interval


    return merged
```

3. Rotating an Array:

- Problem: Given an array, rotate it to the right by a given number of steps kkk.
- Challenge: The brute force approach would involve moving elements one by one, which could be inefficient for large arrays.
- **Optimized Approach:** Instead of rotating one element at a time, reverse parts of the array in-place using the reverse method to achieve an optimal time complexity of $O(n)O(n)O(n)$.

Example:

python

```
def rotate_array(arr, k):
    n = len(arr)
    k = k % n  # In case k is greater than the length of the array
    arr.reverse()  # Reverse the entire array
    arr[:k] = reversed(arr[:k])  # Reverse the first part
    arr[k:] = reversed(arr[k:])  # Reverse the second part
    return arr
```

Optimizing Solutions Using Arrays

Arrays can be solved with a variety of techniques, but ensuring your solution is optimized in terms of time and space complexity is crucial. Here are some strategies for optimizing array solutions:

1. Reducing Time Complexity with Efficient Searching and Sorting:

- In problems that involve searching for elements or finding maximum/minimum values, choosing the right algorithm can significantly reduce time complexity. For example:
  - Use **binary search** for searching in sorted arrays, which has a time complexity of

$O(\log n)O(\log n)O(\log n)$, instead of performing a linear search $(O(n)O(n)O(n))$.

o Use efficient sorting algorithms like **MergeSort** or **QuickSort** (both $O(n\log n)O(n \log n)O(n\log n))$ instead of **Bubble Sort** or **Selection Sort** $(O(n2)O(n^2)O(n2))$.

2. Using Hash Sets or Hash Maps for Faster Lookups:

- In problems where you need to check if an element has been seen before or count occurrences, a **hash set** or **hash map** can provide **constant time lookups** $(O(1)O(1)O(1))$ compared to the linear time complexity $(O(n)O(n)O(n))$ of searching through the array.

3. Using Two Pointers for Space Efficiency:

- The two-pointer technique is a very useful way to optimize space and time complexity when working with arrays. This technique involves having two pointers (or indices) traverse the array from different starting points.

- o **Use case:** Finding pairs in a sorted array that sum to a target value or removing duplicates from a sorted array.

Example:

python

```python
def remove_duplicates(arr):
    if not arr:
        return arr

    # Two-pointer approach
    i = 0  # Pointer for the unique elements
    for j in range(1, len(arr)):
        if arr[i] != arr[j]:
            i += 1
            arr[i] = arr[j]  # Place the unique element at index i

    return arr[:i+1]  # Return the array up to the last unique element
```

4. In-place Modifications:

- Whenever possible, modify the array in place (without using extra space for another array). This saves memory and is an important consideration, especially when working with large datasets.
    - **Example:** Reversing an array, rotating an array, or removing duplicates in a sorted array can often be done in-place.

5. Breaking Down the Problem:

- Large problems involving arrays can often be broken down into smaller, simpler problems. Consider using **divide and conquer**, **dynamic programming**, or **greedy algorithms** when appropriate to solve subproblems and build a solution incrementally.

Real-World Examples and When to Use Each Array Solution

Here are a few real-world scenarios where arrays are commonly used, along with the appropriate techniques for solving them:

1. Finding Duplicates in a Large Dataset (Array of Integers):

- **Problem:** You have a large array of integers, and you need to identify any duplicates.

- **Solution:** Use a **hash set** to track the elements you've already seen and identify duplicates in $O(n)O(n)O(n)$ time.

- **Example:** This is useful in applications like validating user input, detecting repeated entries in a database, or finding duplicate records in a list of transactions.

2. Merging Intervals (Meeting Times, Schedules):

- **Problem:** You are given a list of intervals (start and end times) of meetings or events. You need to merge any overlapping intervals to create a non-overlapping schedule.

- **Solution: Sort the intervals** by start time and merge them in $O(nlogⁿn)O(n \log n)O(nlogn)$ time.

- **Example:** This is applicable in scheduling systems, where you want to combine overlapping meeting times into a free slot for other appointments.

3. Rotating an Array (Image or Data Rotation):

- **Problem:** You need to rotate an array or list of data (e.g., an image or data stream) to the right by a given number of steps.

- **Solution:** Use **in-place reversal** to rotate the array in $O(n)O(n)O(n)$ time, minimizing space complexity.

- **Example:** This can be applied to scenarios like rotating matrices in image processing or cyclically rotating elements in real-time data streams.

4. Sorting Data (Large Datasets in Real-Time Applications):

- **Problem:** You have an array of user records, and you need to sort them based on some criteria (e.g., timestamps, scores).

- **Solution:** Use an efficient sorting algorithm like **MergeSort** or **QuickSort** ($O(n\log n)O(n \log n)O(n\log n)$).

- **Example:** Sorting is commonly used in systems that deal with user-generated content, like organizing posts by time or ranking users by score in a leaderboard.

Conclusion

Arrays are one of the most fundamental data structures in coding interviews, and understanding how to solve problems efficiently with arrays is crucial. From finding duplicates to merging intervals and rotating arrays, the key to success lies in choosing the right approach based on the problem's constraints. By mastering array manipulation techniques, optimizing solutions for time and space complexity, and practicing real-world scenarios, you'll be well-prepared for the array-based problems that come your way in interviews.

CHAPTER 6

MASTERING STRINGS AND TEXT PROCESSING

Strings are one of the most commonly encountered data types in coding interviews, and they are fundamental in solving a wide range of problems. Whether it's manipulating text, searching for specific patterns, or validating input, string-related problems are often central to many coding challenges. In this chapter, we'll cover some common string manipulation problems, techniques to efficiently solve these problems, and real-world examples that demonstrate how to handle strings effectively.

Common String Manipulation Problems in Coding Interviews

String manipulation problems in coding interviews often test your ability to think critically and apply algorithms and data structures effectively. Some common types of string-related problems you may encounter include:

1. Reversing a String:

- Problem: Given a string, reverse its characters.
- This is one of the simplest string manipulation problems but serves as a foundation for more complex tasks like string reversal in data processing or undo operations in applications.

2. Anagram Checking:

- Problem: Given two strings, determine if they are anagrams (i.e., they contain the same characters with the same frequencies).
- Anagrams are often used in algorithms that involve grouping or comparing text-based data.

3. Substring Search:

- Problem: Given a string and a target substring, find the first occurrence of the substring in the string.
- This problem often comes up when working with string matching algorithms, like searching for keywords or finding specific data patterns within large text files.

4. Palindrome Checking:

- Problem: Given a string, check if it reads the same forward and backward.
- Palindrome problems are useful in text validation, like checking for symmetry in DNA sequences or mirrored data in various applications.

5. Longest Substring Without Repeating Characters:

- Problem: Given a string, find the longest substring without repeating characters.
- This type of problem is helpful in analyzing patterns in strings and is particularly important in applications like text compression and encryption.

Techniques for Solving String-Related Problems

When solving string-related problems, it's essential to use efficient algorithms and techniques to avoid unnecessary computations. Below are key techniques you should be familiar with when tackling string manipulation problems:

1. Two-Pointer Technique:

- The **two-pointer technique** is often used in problems where you need to traverse a string or substring and check specific conditions. This technique involves using two pointers to scan the string in a linear fashion, which can reduce time complexity.

- Common use cases include problems like reversing a string, checking for palindromes, and finding substrings.

2. Hash Maps and Hash Sets:

- For problems that require checking the frequency of characters or verifying the uniqueness of characters, **hash maps** or **hash sets** are extremely useful. They allow for **constant time lookups**, making them ideal for anagram checking, character counting, and substring search.
- Using a hash set can help solve problems like checking if characters repeat in a string or finding unique characters.

3. Sliding Window Technique:

- The **sliding window technique** is used for problems that require finding a substring of fixed or variable length, especially when dealing with a large string.

This technique helps maintain a window of elements, adjusting the start and end positions to explore different segments of the string efficiently.

- This is particularly useful for problems like finding the longest substring without repeating characters.

4. In-Place Modifications:

- For problems like reversing strings or removing certain characters from a string, performing in-place modifications helps reduce space complexity. This can be done using two-pointer techniques to swap characters directly within the string.

5. Sorting:

- Sorting can be useful in problems like anagram checking, where sorting the characters of both strings and comparing them can provide a simple and efficient solution.

Real-World Examples: Reversing a String, Anagram Checking, and Substring Search

Let's explore some real-world examples of string manipulation problems and how to solve them efficiently.

1. Reversing a String:

- **Problem:** Given a string, reverse the characters in place.
- **Example:** Input: "hello", Output: "olleh"
- **Approach:** You can use the **two-pointer technique** to reverse the string in place. Start by initializing two pointers, one at the beginning of the string and one at the end, and swap the characters until the pointers meet in the middle.

Solution:

python

```
def reverse_string(s):
    s = list(s)  # Convert string to a list for in-place modification
    left, right = 0, len(s) - 1
    while left < right:
```

```
s[left], s[right] = s[right], s[left]  # Swap characters
left += 1
right -= 1
```
return ".join(s) # Convert the list back to a string

2. Anagram Checking:

- **Problem:** Given two strings, determine if they are anagrams of each other.
- **Example:** Input: "listen", "silent", Output: True
- **Approach:** One way to check if two strings are anagrams is by sorting both strings and comparing them. Alternatively, you can use a **hash map** to count the frequency of each character in both strings and compare the counts.

Solution using sorting:

python

```
def are_anagrams(str1, str2):
    return sorted(str1) == sorted(str2)
```

Solution using hash map:

python

```python
from collections import Counter


def are_anagrams(str1, str2):
    return Counter(str1) == Counter(str2)
```

3. Substring Search:

- **Problem:** Given a string and a target substring, find the first occurrence of the substring within the string.
- **Example:** Input: "hello world", "world", Output: 6 (index where the substring starts)
- **Approach:** The simplest approach is to use the built-in function, but for interview purposes, you can implement an efficient search algorithm like **Knuth-Morris-Pratt (KMP)** or **Rabin-Karp**.

Solution using Python's built-in find:

python

```python
def substring_search(string, substring):
    return string.find(substring)
```

Solution using the sliding window approach (naive implementation):

python

```python
def substring_search(string, substring):
    for i in range(len(string) - len(substring) + 1):
        if string[i:i+len(substring)] == substring:
            return i  # Return index of first occurrence
    return -1  # Return -1 if substring is not found
```

Additional String Manipulation Problems

1. Palindrome Checking:

- **Problem:** Given a string, check if it is a palindrome (reads the same forward and backward).
- **Approach:** This can be solved using the **two-pointer technique**, where one pointer starts at the beginning of the string and the other at the end. If the characters are the same, move the pointers toward the center.

Solution:

python

```python
def is_palindrome(s):
```

78

```
left, right = 0, len(s) - 1
while left < right:
    if s[left] != s[right]:
        return False
    left += 1
    right -= 1
return True
```

2. Longest Substring Without Repeating Characters:

- **Problem:** Given a string, find the length of the longest substring without repeating characters.

- **Approach:** Use the **sliding window technique** with two pointers. Maintain a window of unique characters and adjust the window size as you move the right pointer. Keep track of the maximum length of the window.

Solution:

python

```
def longest_unique_substring(s):
    char_set = set()
    left = 0
```

```
max_length = 0

for right in range(len(s)):
    while s[right] in char_set:
        char_set.remove(s[left])
        left += 1
    char_set.add(s[right])
    max_length = max(max_length, right - left + 1)

return max_length
```

Conclusion

Mastering string manipulation is a critical skill for coding interviews, as many problems are based on string processing. In this chapter, we've covered common string manipulation problems, the techniques used to solve them efficiently, and real-world examples. By practicing these problems and techniques, you'll be well-prepared to tackle string-related challenges in coding interviews and apply these skills in various real-world applications, from text parsing to pattern recognition.

CHAPTER 7

LINKED LISTS: NAVIGATING NODES AND POINTERS

Linked lists are one of the most fundamental and versatile data structures in computer science. They are used in a wide range of applications, from memory management to implementing complex algorithms. In this chapter, we'll dive into the two main types of linked lists—singly and doubly linked lists—understand their characteristics, explore common problems and techniques for manipulating linked lists, and go through real-world examples like reversing a linked list, detecting loops, and merging sorted lists.

Understanding Singly and Doubly Linked Lists

A **linked list** is a linear data structure where elements, called **nodes**, are stored in a sequence, and each node points to the next node in the list. This provides flexibility in adding and removing elements at different positions in the list without the need for contiguous memory allocation.

1. Singly Linked List:

- A **singly linked list** consists of nodes where each node contains two parts:
  - **Data**: The value stored in the node.
  - **Next Pointer**: A reference to the next node in the list.
- The last node in a singly linked list has a **null** reference for the next pointer, indicating the end of the list.

Structure:

rust

Node1 -> Node2 -> Node3 -> Null

Operations:

- **Insertion**: Adding a node at the beginning, end, or at a specific position.
- **Deletion**: Removing a node by value or position.
- **Traversal**: Visiting each node in the list.

2. Doubly Linked List:

- A **doubly linked list** is a variation where each node contains three parts:
  - **Data**: The value stored in the node.
  - **Next Pointer**: A reference to the next node.
  - **Previous Pointer**: A reference to the previous node.
- This allows for traversal in both directions, forward and backward.

Structure:

rust

Null <- Node1 <-> Node2 <-> Node3 -> Null

Operations:

- **Insertion and Deletion**: Same as singly linked lists, but with more flexibility since each node has references to both its previous and next node.
- **Traversal**: Can be done in both directions, making it easier to navigate backward.

Common Problems and Techniques for Linked List Manipulation

Linked lists are often used to implement a variety of algorithms and can be manipulated in many ways. Here are some common problems and techniques used for manipulating linked lists:

1. Reversing a Linked List:

- Problem: Given a singly linked list, reverse the list so that the first node becomes the last and vice versa.
- **Approach:** Traverse the list while reversing the **next pointers**. For each node, point its **next** to the previous node, and move the pointers forward.

Solution (Singly Linked List):

python

```python
class ListNode:
    def __init__(self, value=0, next=None):
        self.value = value
        self.next = next


def reverse_linked_list(head):
```

```
prev = None
current = head


while current:
    next_node = current.next  # Save the next node
    current.next = prev       # Reverse the link
    prev = current            # Move prev and current forward
    current = next_node


return prev  # New head of the reversed list
```

2. Detecting Loops in a Linked List:

- Problem: Given a singly linked list, determine if there is a cycle (loop) in the list. A cycle occurs when a node's **next** pointer points to a previous node in the list, creating a loop.

- **Approach:** Use the **Floyd's Tortoise and Hare Algorithm** (two pointers: one moves slow, one moves fast). If there's a cycle, the two pointers will meet at some point. If the fast pointer reaches the end of the list (null), there's no cycle.

Solution:

python

```python
def has_cycle(head):
    slow = head
    fast = head

    while fast and fast.next:
        slow = slow.next          # Move slow pointer by one step
        fast = fast.next.next     # Move fast pointer by two steps

        if slow == fast:          # Cycle detected
            return True

    return False  # No cycle
```

3. Merging Two Sorted Linked Lists:

- Problem: Given two sorted linked lists, merge them into a single sorted list.
- **Approach:** Compare the nodes of the two lists, and iteratively add the smaller node to the new list. This can be done efficiently in linear time by keeping track of the current node in each list.

Solution:

python

```
def merge_sorted_lists(l1, l2):
    dummy = ListNode()   # A dummy node to start the merged list
    current = dummy

    while l1 and l2:
        if l1.value < l2.value:
            current.next = l1
            l1 = l1.next
        else:
            current.next = l2
            l2 = l2.next
        current = current.next  # Move to the next node

    # If any nodes remain in either list, append them
    current.next = l1 if l1 else l2

    return dummy.next  # Return the head of the merged list
```

Real-World Examples: Reversing a Linked List, Detecting Loops, and Merging Sorted Lists

Let's take a look at how these linked list problems apply to real-world use cases:

1. Reversing a Linked List:

- **Real-World Example:** Reversing a singly linked list is often used in applications where the order of elements needs to be reversed, such as reversing the history of web pages in a browser's back button or implementing undo operations in text editors.

- **Application:** Reversing the sequence of elements in a playlist or a set of tasks.

2. Detecting Loops in a Linked List:

- **Real-World Example:** Detecting loops is crucial in network routing, where packets might get stuck in an infinite loop, causing delays or system crashes. In programming, cycle detection is used to prevent infinite loops or recursive calls in linked data structures.

- **Application:** Detecting cyclic dependencies in a dependency graph (e.g., project tasks or software modules) to avoid deadlocks or infinite loops.

3. Merging Sorted Lists:

- **Real-World Example:** Merging sorted lists is commonly used in applications that handle large datasets, like **merging log files** from different servers, or combining search results from different sources.

- **Application:** Combining sorted customer transaction records from two different databases to create a consolidated, sorted list of all transactions.

Conclusion

Linked lists are a crucial data structure in coding interviews, especially for problems that involve dynamic memory allocation or require efficient insertion and deletion of nodes. Understanding both singly and doubly linked lists, and knowing how to manipulate them efficiently, will help you solve a wide range of problems in coding interviews. In this chapter, we covered common linked list manipulation techniques, including reversing a list, detecting cycles, and merging sorted lists, along with real-world examples of how these techniques are applied in various applications. By mastering these operations, you'll be well-prepared for the linked list problems you might encounter in your next interview.

CHAPTER 8

STACKS AND QUEUES: ORGANIZING DATA

Stacks and queues are two of the most important abstract data types in computer science, widely used in various algorithms and applications. Both play critical roles in organizing and managing data in a way that enables efficient processing. Understanding how they work, and when to use them, is crucial for solving many coding problems, especially in tech interviews. In this chapter, we'll explore the concepts of stacks and queues, solve problems using these data structures, and provide real-world examples where they are commonly applied.

What are Stacks and Queues and Why Are They Important?

1. Stacks:

- A **stack** is a linear data structure that follows the **Last In First Out (LIFO)** principle, meaning the last element added is the first one to be removed. This

91

behavior can be likened to a stack of plates where you add new plates to the top and remove plates from the top.

- **Operations on Stacks:**
  - **Push**: Add an element to the top of the stack.
  - **Pop**: Remove the top element from the stack.
  - **Peek/Top**: View the element at the top of the stack without removing it.
  - **IsEmpty**: Check if the stack is empty.

Applications of Stacks:

- **Undo functionality**: Many applications (e.g., text editors) use stacks to manage undo actions, where the most recent action is undone first.
- **Expression evaluation**: Stacks are used to evaluate expressions in postfix or prefix notation.
- **Depth-First Search (DFS)**: In graph traversal, stacks help explore nodes in a DFS approach.

2. Queues:

- A **queue** is a linear data structure that follows the **First In First Out (FIFO)** principle, meaning the first element added is the first one to be removed. A queue is like a line at a ticket counter where the first person to arrive is the first to be served.

- **Operations on Queues:**
    - o **Enqueue**: Add an element to the back of the queue.
    - o **Dequeue**: Remove the front element from the queue.
    - o **Front/Peek**: View the element at the front of the queue without removing it.
    - o **IsEmpty**: Check if the queue is empty.

Applications of Queues:

- **Task scheduling**: Queues are used in operating systems to manage processes waiting for execution.
- **Breadth-First Search (BFS)**: In graph traversal, queues help explore nodes level by level in a BFS approach.
- **Buffer management**: Queues are used in managing data buffers in networking and IO operations, such as message queues and print queues.

Solving Problems with Stacks and Queues

Both stacks and queues provide an organized way to process elements in a defined order. Below, we will look at common problems that are efficiently solved using stacks and queues.

1. Balanced Parentheses:

- **Problem:** Given a string containing parentheses (e.g., (), {}, []), determine if the parentheses are balanced. A string is balanced if every opening parenthesis has a corresponding closing parenthesis, and they are properly nested.

- **Solution:** This problem can be solved using a stack. Traverse the string, and for each opening parenthesis ('(', '{', '['), push it onto the stack. For each closing parenthesis (')', '}', ']'), check if it matches the top of the stack. If they match, pop the top of the stack; otherwise, return false. If the stack is empty at the end, the parentheses are balanced.

Solution:

python

```
def is_balanced(s):
```

```
stack = []
mapping = {')': '(', '}': '{', ']': '['}

for char in s:
    if char in mapping:  # If it's a closing bracket
        top_element = stack.pop() if stack else '#'
        if mapping[char] != top_element:
            return False
    else:
        stack.append(char)  # If it's an opening bracket

return not stack  # Stack should be empty if balanced
```

2. Queue Simulation:

- **Problem:** Simulate the behavior of a queue. For example, consider a queue of people waiting for service at a counter. People arrive at different times, and the first person in line is served first. This problem can be simulated using a queue.

- **Solution:** Use a queue to simulate the arrival of people and their processing. Enqueue new arrivals and dequeue the person at the front when they are served.

Solution:

python

```python
class Queue:
    def __init__(self):
        self.queue = []

    def enqueue(self, item):
        self.queue.append(item)

    def dequeue(self):
        if self.is_empty():
            return "Queue is empty"
        return self.queue.pop(0)

    def is_empty(self):
        return len(self.queue) == 0

# Example usage:
queue = Queue()
queue.enqueue("Person 1")
queue.enqueue("Person 2")
print(queue.dequeue())  # Output: Person 1
```

3. Implementing a Stack Using Two Queues:

- **Problem:** Implement a stack using two queues. A stack operates on the **LIFO** principle, but you are restricted to using queues, which operate on the **FIFO** principle.

- **Solution:** One approach to implement a stack using two queues is to always make sure that the most recently added element is at the front of one of the queues. Every time an element is pushed, it's enqueued in one queue. When popping an element, move all elements except the last one to the other queue, and dequeue the last element.

Solution:

python

```
from queue import Queue


class StackUsingQueues:
    def __init__(self):
        self.queue1 = Queue()
        self.queue2 = Queue()
```

```
def push(self, x):
    self.queue1.put(x)


def pop(self):
    if self.queue1.empty():
        return None
    # Move elements from queue1 to queue2, leaving the
last element in queue1
    while self.queue1.qsize() > 1:
        self.queue2.put(self.queue1.get())


    # The last element in queue1 is the top of the stack
    top_element = self.queue1.get()


    # Swap the two queues
    self.queue1, self.queue2 = self.queue2, self.queue1


    return top_element

# Example usage:
stack = StackUsingQueues()
stack.push(1)
stack.push(2)
print(stack.pop())  # Output: 2
```

Real-World Examples of Stacks and Queues

1. Balanced Parentheses:

- **Real-World Example:** This problem is commonly encountered in compilers and parsers that need to validate the syntax of expressions. Balancing parentheses ensures that expressions are correctly structured.

- **Application:** Used in mathematical expression evaluators or when verifying code syntax in compilers.

2. Queue Simulation:

- **Real-World Example:** This scenario is applicable in systems where requests or tasks are processed in the order they arrive, such as job scheduling in operating systems, printer queues, or customer service systems.

- **Application:** Used to model real-time systems where tasks or requests are handled sequentially, like managing print jobs or processing requests in web servers.

3. Implementing a Stack with Two Queues:

- **Real-World Example:** This can be useful in scenarios where you need to implement a stack in a system that only has access to a queue-based data structure, or in situations where you want to simulate a stack using queue operations for testing purposes.

- **Application:** A good example of this is in distributed systems where one queue is used for incoming data and the other for processing.

Conclusion

Stacks and queues are essential data structures that allow you to efficiently manage data in a defined order. Understanding how to implement and manipulate these data structures is crucial for solving various types of problems in coding interviews. In this chapter, we've explored the concepts of stacks and queues, common problems like balancing parentheses, queue simulations, and stack implementations using two queues. By mastering these data structures and their applications, you will be well-equipped to solve a wide range of algorithmic challenges in interviews and real-world systems.

CHAPTER 9

TREES AND GRAPHS - BUILDING HIERARCHIES

Trees and graphs are fundamental data structures that are widely used to represent hierarchical structures and relationships. Whether it's building a family tree, managing file systems, or representing networks in a computer, understanding how to work with trees and graphs is crucial for solving complex problems in coding interviews and real-world applications. In this chapter, we'll explore binary trees, binary search trees, and graphs, dive into traversal techniques and graph algorithms, and examine real-world examples where these structures are commonly used.

Understanding Binary Trees, Binary Search Trees, and Graphs

1. Binary Trees:

- A **binary tree** is a tree where each node has at most two children, referred to as the **left** and **right** child.

The topmost node is called the **root**. Binary trees are used in many applications, such as representing hierarchical data or constructing decision trees.

Properties:

- Each node has at most two children.
- The height of the tree is the number of edges on the longest path from the root to a leaf.

Example of a Binary Tree:

markdown

```
   1
  / \
 2   3
/ \
4   5
```

2. Binary Search Trees (BST):

- A **binary search tree** is a special type of binary tree where the left child of a node contains only values less than the node's value, and the right child contains values greater than the node's value. This property makes searching for values in a BST much more efficient than in an unsorted binary tree.

Properties:

- Left child < Parent node < Right child
- This property allows for efficient searching, insertion, and deletion.

Example of a Binary Search Tree:

markdown

```
  10
 / \
5  15
/\  \
3 7  20
```

3. Graphs:

- A **graph** is a non-linear data structure consisting of a set of nodes (vertices) connected by edges. Graphs can represent many types of real-world relationships, such as social networks, web page connections, or transportation systems.

- **Directed vs. Undirected**: In **directed graphs**, edges have a direction (from one node to another), while in **undirected graphs**, edges have no direction.
- **Weighted vs. Unweighted**: In **weighted graphs**, edges have weights (or costs) associated with them, whereas in **unweighted graphs**, all edges are considered equal.

Example of a Graph:

less

```
A -- B
|    |
D -- C
```

Tree Traversal Techniques: Inorder, Preorder, and Postorder

Tree traversal refers to the process of visiting all the nodes in a tree in a specific order. Traversal is essential for performing operations like searching, updating, or deleting nodes in a tree.

1. Inorder Traversal (Left, Root, Right):

- Visit the left subtree, then the root node, and finally the right subtree.
- In a binary search tree, an **inorder traversal** visits nodes in ascending order.

Example (Inorder Traversal):

markdown

```
    1
   / \
  2   3
 / \
4   5
```

Inorder Traversal: 4, 2, 5, 1, 3

Code:

python

```python
def inorder(root):
    if root:
        inorder(root.left)
        print(root.value)
        inorder(root.right)
```

2. Preorder Traversal (Root, Left, Right):

- Visit the root node first, then the left subtree, and finally the right subtree.

Example (Preorder Traversal):

markdown

```
   1
  / \
 2   3
/ \
4  5
```

Preorder Traversal: 1, 2, 4, 5, 3

Code:

python

```
def preorder(root):
    if root:
        print(root.value)
        preorder(root.left)
        preorder(root.right)
```

3. Postorder Traversal (Left, Right, Root):

- Visit the left subtree first, then the right subtree, and finally the root node.

Example (Postorder Traversal):

markdown

```
    1
   / \
  2   3
 / \
4   5
```

Postorder Traversal: 4, 5, 2, 3, 1

Code:

python

```
def postorder(root):
    if root:
        postorder(root.left)
        postorder(root.right)
        print(root.value)
```

Graph Algorithms: BFS (Breadth-First Search) and DFS (Depth-First Search)

Graphs are versatile and can be traversed using different algorithms, depending on the problem you're trying to solve. Two of the most popular graph traversal techniques are **Breadth-First Search (BFS)** and **Depth-First Search (DFS)**.

1. Breadth-First Search (BFS):

- **BFS** explores all the neighbors of a node before moving on to the next level. It uses a **queue** to explore nodes level by level.
- **BFS** is typically used to find the shortest path in an unweighted graph or to explore nodes in the order of their distance from the starting node.

Example (BFS Traversal):

mathematica

```
    A
   / \
```

109

```
  B   C
 /\  \
D  E  F
```

BFS Traversal: A, B, C, D, E, F

Code:

python

```python
from collections import deque

def bfs(graph, start):
    visited = set()
    queue = deque([start])

    while queue:
        node = queue.popleft()
        if node not in visited:
            print(node)
            visited.add(node)
            queue.extend(graph[node])  # Add neighbors to the queue
```

2. Depth-First Search (DFS):

- **DFS** explores as far as possible along each branch before backtracking. It can be implemented using either **recursion** or an **explicit stack**.
- **DFS** is often used for tasks like topological sorting or finding connected components in a graph.

Example (DFS Traversal):

mathematica

```
  A
 / \
 B   C
/ \   \
D E   F
```

DFS Traversal: A, B, D, E, C, F

Code (Recursive DFS):

python

```python
def dfs(graph, node, visited=None):
    if visited is None:
        visited = set()
    visited.add(node)
```

```
print(node)
for neighbor in graph[node]:
    if neighbor not in visited:
        dfs(graph, neighbor, visited)
```

Real-World Examples: Finding the Shortest Path, Tree Traversal, and Topological Sorting

1. Finding the Shortest Path:

- **Problem:** In a graph representing a network, find the shortest path between two nodes.
- **Application:** In networking, BFS is used to find the shortest path between two nodes in an unweighted graph, such as routing packets through a network.
- **Solution:** Use **BFS** for unweighted graphs or **Dijkstra's algorithm** for weighted graphs to find the shortest path between nodes.

2. Tree Traversal (Inorder, Preorder, Postorder):

- **Problem:** Traversing a tree to print all the nodes in a particular order.
- **Application:** In binary search trees, **inorder traversal** is used to retrieve the elements in

ascending order. This is essential for sorting algorithms or searching operations in databases.

- **Solution:** Use **inorder, preorder,** or **postorder** traversal depending on the application.

3. Topological Sorting:

- **Problem:** Given a directed graph, return the vertices in a linear order such that for every directed edge uvuvuv, vertex uuu comes before vertex vvv.
- **Application:** Topological sorting is used in tasks like job scheduling, where certain tasks must be performed before others.
- **Solution:** Use **DFS** to find the topological order of a directed acyclic graph (DAG).

Code for Topological Sorting:

python

```python
def topological_sort(graph):
    visited = set()
    result = []

    def dfs(node):
```

```
        if node not in visited:
            visited.add(node)
            for neighbor in graph[node]:
                dfs(neighbor)
            result.append(node)


    for node in graph:
        if node not in visited:
            dfs(node)


    return result[::-1]   # Reverse the result to get the
topological order
```

Conclusion

Understanding trees and graphs is essential for solving a wide range of problems in coding interviews and real-world applications. In this chapter, we explored the concepts of **binary trees**, **binary search trees**, and **graphs**, and discussed important traversal techniques such as **inorder**, **preorder**, and **postorder** for trees. Additionally, we covered **BFS** and **DFS** graph traversal algorithms, which are widely used in problems like finding the shortest path, tree traversal, and topological sorting. By mastering these concepts, you'll be well-equipped to tackle more complex problems and build efficient solutions using trees and graphs.

CHAPTER 10

HASHING AND HASH MAPS - FAST LOOKUPS

Hashing is one of the most powerful techniques used in computer science for solving problems efficiently, especially when it comes to **fast lookups** and **data retrieval**. **Hash maps** (or hash tables) utilize hashing to provide constant-time average complexity for operations like insertion, deletion, and searching. In this chapter, we will delve into the concepts of hashing and hash maps, explore how to solve common problems efficiently using hash maps, and look at real-world examples that highlight the importance of hashing.

Understanding Hashing and Hash Maps

1. Hashing:

- **Hashing** is a technique used to uniquely map data (usually a key) to a fixed-size value (often an index or a hash code) through a hash function. This allows for very efficient data storage and retrieval.

- A **hash function** takes in a key (e.g., a string or integer) and returns a corresponding index in a hash table. The goal of a good hash function is to distribute the keys uniformly across the hash table to minimize the occurrence of **collisions** (when two keys map to the same index).

Example:

- Suppose we have a hash function that maps the string "apple" to the index 5. If "apple" is inserted into the hash map, it will be stored at index 5.

2. Hash Maps (Hash Tables):

- A **hash map** (or **hash table**) is a data structure that stores key-value pairs. It uses a hash function to compute an index (or hash code) for a key, and stores the corresponding value at that index.
- Hash maps offer **constant time complexity O(1)O(1)O(1)** for the basic operations like **insertion, deletion**, and **lookup**, on average.

Example:

- A hash map can store a person's **name** as the key and their **phone number** as the value. Using the name (key), you can efficiently retrieve the phone number (value).

Basic Operations:

- **Put (Insert):** Adds a key-value pair to the hash map.
- **Get (Retrieve):** Retrieves the value associated with a given key.
- **Remove:** Deletes a key-value pair from the hash map.
- **ContainsKey:** Checks if a key exists in the hash map.

Key Benefits:

- Fast lookups and insertions.
- Efficient searching for specific data based on a key.

Solving Problems Efficiently Using Hash Maps

Hash maps are powerful tools for solving a wide variety of algorithmic problems efficiently. Here are some common problems that are best solved using hash maps:

1. Counting Frequencies:

- **Problem:** Given an array of elements, count the frequency of each element.
- **Solution:** You can use a hash map where the keys are the array elements and the values are the counts of their occurrences. This allows you to count frequencies in **linear time O(n)O(n)O(n)**.

Example: Counting word frequencies in a text file or counting characters in a string.

Code:

python

```python
def count_frequencies(arr):
    freq_map = {}
    for item in arr:
        if item in freq_map:
            freq_map[item] += 1
        else:
            freq_map[item] = 1
    return freq_map
```

```python
# Example usage:
arr = ['a', 'b', 'a', 'c', 'a', 'b']
print(count_frequencies(arr))  # Output: {'a': 3, 'b': 2, 'c': 1}
```

2. Finding Pairs that Sum to a Target:

- **Problem:** Given an array of integers, find all pairs of numbers that sum to a target value.
- **Solution:** Using a hash map, you can store the elements you've already visited. For each element in the array, check if the complement (target - current element) exists in the hash map. This allows you to find pairs in **linear time O(n)O(n)O(n)**.

Example: Finding pairs of numbers that sum to a target value in a list of integers.

Code:

python

```python
def find_pairs(arr, target):
    seen = set()
    pairs = []
    for num in arr:
        complement = target - num
```

```
    if complement in seen:
        pairs.append((complement, num))
    seen.add(num)
    return pairs
```

```
# Example usage:
arr = [1, 2, 3, 4, 5]
target = 5
print(find_pairs(arr, target))  # Output: [(2, 3), (1, 4)]
```

3. Solving Anagrams:

- **Problem:** Given two strings, check if they are anagrams of each other. Two strings are anagrams if they contain the same characters with the same frequencies, but possibly in a different order.
- **Solution:** You can use a hash map (or hash set) to store the frequency of each character in both strings. If the frequency distributions match, the strings are anagrams.

Example: Checking if two strings are anagrams of each other, such as "listen" and "silent".

Code:

python

```python
def are_anagrams(str1, str2):
    if len(str1) != len(str2):
        return False
    count_map = {}
    for char in str1:
        count_map[char] = count_map.get(char, 0) + 1
    for char in str2:
        if char not in count_map or count_map[char] == 0:
            return False
        count_map[char] -= 1
    return True


# Example usage:
print(are_anagrams("listen", "silent"))  # Output: True
print(are_anagrams("hello", "world"))   # Output: False
```

Real-World Examples of Hashing and Hash Maps

Hash maps are widely used in real-world applications due to their efficient lookup, insertion, and deletion properties. Below are some examples of how hash maps are applied in practice:

1. Counting Frequencies:

- **Application:** In text processing, hash maps are used to count the frequency of words or characters. For example, word count tools in text editors or search engines use hash maps to track the frequency of words in documents, helping rank them based on how often certain terms appear.
- **Use Case:** Searching for frequently occurring keywords in large text documents or logs.

2. Finding Pairs that Sum to a Target:

- **Application:** Hash maps are used in financial applications to detect pairs of transactions that sum to a target value (e.g., finding pairs of investment opportunities that meet a certain target return).
- **Use Case:** In data analytics, hash maps can help identify pairs of values or records that meet certain criteria, such as identifying matching transactions or correlated items in a recommendation system.

3. Solving Anagrams:

- **Application:** Hash maps are used to solve problems related to text comparison, such as checking if two words are anagrams, sorting strings, or organizing words into groups of anagrams. This technique is used in search engines, social media platforms, and large-scale text processing tools.

- **Use Case:** Organizing a dictionary of words into groups of anagrams or building anagrams-based search features for an online platform.

Conclusion

Hashing and hash maps are powerful tools for solving many algorithmic problems with excellent time efficiency. They allow for **constant-time lookups** and are crucial in applications that require fast data retrieval or manipulation. In this chapter, we covered fundamental problems such as counting frequencies, finding pairs that sum to a target, and solving anagram problems, all of which can be efficiently solved using hash maps. Real-world applications of hash maps include text processing, data analytics, financial transactions, and many other fields. Mastering the use of hash maps will enable you to solve complex problems with ease and optimize the performance of your algorithms in coding interviews and real-world projects.

CHAPTER 11

RECURSION AND BACKTRACKING - BREAKING DOWN PROBLEMS

Recursion and backtracking are powerful problem-solving techniques used to break down complex problems into simpler subproblems, and are particularly useful in scenarios where multiple potential solutions need to be explored. In this chapter, we will delve into the concepts of recursion and backtracking, explain how to approach problems using these techniques, and go over real-world examples such as solving the N-Queens problem, generating subsets, and generating permutations.

Introduction to Recursion and Backtracking

1. Recursion:

- **Recursion** is a programming technique in which a function calls itself to solve smaller instances of the same problem. It is often used in problems that can be broken down into smaller, similar subproblems, such as navigating through trees or solving mathematical sequences.

- A recursive solution typically involves:
    - A **base case**: The condition under which the function stops calling itself.
    - A **recursive case**: The part of the function where the function calls itself to solve a smaller subproblem.

Example:

- The classic example of recursion is computing the **factorial** of a number, where n! = n * (n-1)!, with the base case being 1! = 1.

python

```
def factorial(n):
    if n == 0:  # Base case
        return 1
    return n * factorial(n-1)  # Recursive case
```

2. Backtracking:

- **Backtracking** is a refinement of recursion where you explore all possible solutions to a problem by trying partial solutions and abandoning them if they lead to dead ends. It's used for optimization problems, constraint satisfaction, or generating all possible configurations.

- Backtracking works by trying to build the solution incrementally, and if a solution doesn't work, it backtracks to a previous step to try a different path.

Example:

- Backtracking is commonly used in problems like the **N-Queens problem**, where we need to place queens on a chessboard such that no two queens threaten each other.

How to Approach Problems Recursively

When approaching a problem recursively, there are a few important steps to follow:

1. Understand the Problem:

- Break down the problem and check if it has smaller subproblems that are similar to the original problem. Recursion is most effective when the problem can be divided into smaller versions of itself.
- **Example:** In the case of calculating the factorial of a number, the problem breaks down into smaller subproblems (e.g., finding n! involves finding (n-1)!).

2. Define the Base Case:

- Every recursive function must have a base case that stops the recursion. This is crucial to prevent infinite recursion and stack overflow errors.

3. Define the Recursive Case:

- Break the problem down into simpler subproblems and make a recursive call. Each recursive step should work towards reaching the base case.

4. Solve the Problem:

- Implement the recursive function by considering both the base case and the recursive case. Ensure the recursive calls gradually bring the problem closer to the base case.

Real-World Examples: Solving the N-Queens Problem, Subset Generation, and Generating Permutations

Let's explore some real-world problems where recursion and backtracking are commonly used.

1. Solving the N-Queens Problem:

- **Problem:** The N-Queens problem involves placing N queens on an NxN chessboard so that no two queens threaten each other. Queens can attack in rows, columns, and diagonals.
- **Approach:** Use backtracking to try placing queens in each column. If placing a queen leads to a conflict, backtrack and try the next position.

Solution (Backtracking Approach):

python

```python
def is_safe(board, row, col, n):
    for i in range(col):
```

```python
        if board[row][i] == 1:
            return False
    for i, j in zip(range(row, -1, -1), range(col, -1, -1)):
        if board[i][j] == 1:
            return False
    for i, j in zip(range(row, n, 1), range(col, -1, -1)):
        if board[i][j] == 1:
            return False
    return True


def solve_n_queens_util(board, col, n):
    if col >= n:
        return True
    for i in range(n):
        if is_safe(board, i, col, n):
            board[i][col] = 1
            if solve_n_queens_util(board, col + 1, n):
                return True
            board[i][col] = 0  # Backtrack
    return False


def solve_n_queens(n):
    board = [[0] * n for _ in range(n)]
    if solve_n_queens_util(board, 0, n):
```

```python
    return board
    return None


# Example usage
n = 4
solution = solve_n_queens(n)
if solution:
    for row in solution:
        print(row)
```

2. Subset Generation:

- **Problem:** Given a set of numbers, generate all possible subsets (the powerset).
- **Approach:** Use recursion to decide whether to include each element in the subset. At each step, we have two choices: include the current element or exclude it.

Solution (Recursive Approach):

python

```python
def generate_subsets(nums):
    def backtrack(start, path):
```

```
    result.append(path[:])
    for i in range(start, len(nums)):
        path.append(nums[i])
        backtrack(i + 1, path)
        path.pop()


    result = []
    backtrack(0, [])
    return result


# Example usage
nums = [1, 2, 3]
subsets = generate_subsets(nums)
print(subsets)  # Output: [[], [1], [1, 2], [1, 2, 3], [1, 3], [2],
[2, 3], [3]]
```

3. Generating Permutations:

- **Problem:** Given a set of distinct integers, generate all possible permutations of the set.
- **Approach:** Use recursion and backtracking to build all permutations by swapping elements in the array. Once all elements are placed, a complete permutation is formed.

Solution (Backtracking Approach):

python

```
def permute(nums):
    def backtrack(start):
        if start == len(nums):
            result.append(nums[:])
            return
        for i in range(start, len(nums)):
            nums[start], nums[i] = nums[i], nums[start]  # Swap
            backtrack(start + 1)
            nums[start], nums[i] = nums[i], nums[start]  # Undo
the swap (backtrack)

    result = []
    backtrack(0)
    return result


# Example usage
nums = [1, 2, 3]
permutations = permute(nums)
print(permutations)  # Output: [[1, 2, 3], [1, 3, 2], [2, 1, 3],
[2, 3, 1], [3, 1, 2], [3, 2, 1]]
```

Conclusion

Recursion and backtracking are essential tools in a programmer's problem-solving toolkit, especially when tackling complex problems that involve exploring multiple potential solutions. In this chapter, we've explored the core concepts of recursion and backtracking, examined how to approach problems recursively, and walked through real-world examples such as solving the **N-Queens problem**, **generating subsets**, and **generating permutations**. Mastering recursion and backtracking will not only improve your ability to solve algorithmic challenges but also help you design solutions for problems that require exploring all possibilities and choosing the optimal one.

CHAPTER 12

DYNAMIC PROGRAMMING - OPTIMIZING SOLUTIONS

Dynamic programming (DP) is a powerful technique used to solve problems that involve making a series of decisions. It is often employed when a problem can be broken down into overlapping subproblems that can be solved independently. By storing the results of solved subproblems and reusing them, dynamic programming eliminates redundant calculations and significantly improves the efficiency of solutions. In this chapter, we'll explore dynamic programming, how it differs from recursion, and tackle some common dynamic programming problems. We will also look at real-world examples where dynamic programming can be used to optimize solutions.

Understanding Dynamic Programming and How It Differs from Recursion

1. Recursion vs. Dynamic Programming:

- **Recursion** is a technique in which a function calls itself to solve a smaller instance of the same problem. While recursion is useful for solving problems that can be broken into smaller subproblems, it is often inefficient for problems with overlapping subproblems. This is because recursion may recompute the same subproblems multiple times, leading to unnecessary computations.

- **Dynamic programming** is a technique that improves the efficiency of recursive solutions by storing the results of subproblems (either through **memoization** or **tabulation**) and reusing these results when needed. This avoids redundant calculations and ensures that each subproblem is solved only once.

Memoization involves solving a subproblem once and storing the result in a data structure (usually a dictionary or array) so that future calls to the same subproblem can retrieve the result in constant time.

Tabulation involves solving the problem iteratively, filling out a table (or array) in a bottom-up manner. This approach avoids the overhead of recursion and is often more space-efficient.

Example:

- **Recursive Fibonacci:**

python

```
def fibonacci(n):
    if n <= 1:
        return n
    return fibonacci(n-1) + fibonacci(n-2)
```

- **Dynamic Programming (Memoization) Fibonacci:**

python

```
def fibonacci(n, memo={}):
    if n <= 1:
        return n
    if n not in memo:
        memo[n] = fibonacci(n-1, memo) + fibonacci(n-2, memo)
    return memo[n]
```

Common Dynamic Programming Problems

Dynamic programming is commonly used to solve optimization problems where a decision at one step depends on previous decisions. Below are some classic problems that can be solved using dynamic programming:

1. Knapsack Problem:

- **Problem:** Given a set of items, each with a weight and a value, determine the maximum value you can obtain by packing items into a knapsack with a fixed weight capacity.

- **Approach:** Use a 2D table where dp[i][w] represents the maximum value that can be achieved with the first i items and a knapsack capacity of w. The decision is whether to include an item in the knapsack or exclude it based on its weight and value.

Solution:

python

```
def knapsack(weights, values, capacity):
    n = len(weights)
    dp = [[0] * (capacity + 1) for _ in range(n + 1)]
```

138

```
for i in range(1, n + 1):
    for w in range(1, capacity + 1):
        if weights[i - 1] <= w:
            dp[i][w] = max(values[i - 1] + dp[i - 1][w - weights[i - 1]], dp[i - 1][w])
        else:
            dp[i][w] = dp[i - 1][w]


return dp[n][capacity]
```

- **Time Complexity:** $O(n \times W)O(n \times W)O(n \times W)$, where nnn is the number of items and WWW is the weight capacity.

2. Longest Common Subsequence (LCS):

- **Problem:** Given two sequences, find the length of the longest subsequence that is common to both sequences. The subsequence does not need to be contiguous but must maintain the relative order of elements.

- **Approach:** Use a 2D table dp[i][j] where dp[i][j] represents the length of the LCS of the first i characters of the first string and the first j characters of the second string. If the characters at i and j match, we add 1 to the LCS length of the previous subproblem.

Solution:

python

```python
def lcs(str1, str2):
    m, n = len(str1), len(str2)
    dp = [[0] * (n + 1) for _ in range(m + 1)]

    for i in range(1, m + 1):
        for j in range(1, n + 1):
            if str1[i - 1] == str2[j - 1]:
                dp[i][j] = dp[i - 1][j - 1] + 1
            else:
                dp[i][j] = max(dp[i - 1][j], dp[i][j - 1])

    return dp[m][n]
```

- **Time Complexity:** $O(m \times n) O(m \times n) O(m \times n)$, where mmm and nnn are the lengths of the two strings.

3. Fibonacci Sequence:

- **Problem:** Find the nth Fibonacci number, where the Fibonacci sequence is defined as $F(0)=0 F(0) = 0 F(0)=0$, $F(1)=1 F(1) = 1 F(1)=1$, and $F(n)=F(n-1)+F(n-2) F(n) = F(n-1) + F(n-2) F(n)=F(n-1)+F(n-2)$.

- **Approach:** Use dynamic programming (either memoization or tabulation) to store the intermediate results of the Fibonacci sequence.

Solution (Tabulation):

python

```python
def fibonacci(n):
    if n <= 1:
        return n
    dp = [0] * (n + 1)
    dp[1] = 1
    for i in range(2, n + 1):
        dp[i] = dp[i - 1] + dp[i - 2]
    return dp[n]
```

- **Time Complexity:** $O(n)O(n)O(n)$, where nnn is the input number.

Real-World Examples of Dynamic Programming

Dynamic programming can be used in a variety of real-world applications, especially when the problem involves making decisions at each step that depend on previous decisions.

1. Maximum Subarray Sum (Kadane's Algorithm):

- **Problem:** Given an array of integers, find the contiguous subarray with the maximum sum.
- **Approach:** Use dynamic programming to solve this problem by maintaining the maximum sum up to the current index. The decision at each step is whether to include the current element in the existing subarray or start a new subarray.

Solution (Kadane's Algorithm):

python

```python
def max_subarray_sum(nums):
    max_so_far = max_ending_here = nums[0]
```

```
for num in nums[1:]:
    max_ending_here = max(num, max_ending_here +
num)
    max_so_far = max(max_so_far, max_ending_here)
    return max_so_far
```

- **Time Complexity:** $O(n)O(n)O(n)$, where nnn is the length of the array.

2. Coin Change Problem:

- **Problem:** Given a set of coin denominations and a target amount, find the minimum number of coins needed to make the target amount.
- **Approach:** Use dynamic programming to solve this problem by maintaining an array dp[i] that represents the minimum number of coins required to make amount i. The transition involves considering the current coin denomination and checking the minimum coins needed for each sub-amount.

Solution:

python

```
def coin_change(coins, amount):
```

143

```
dp = [float('inf')] * (amount + 1)
dp[0] = 0
for coin in coins:
    for i in range(coin, amount + 1):
        dp[i] = min(dp[i], dp[i - coin] + 1)
return dp[amount] if dp[amount] != float('inf') else -1
```

- **Time Complexity:** $O(n \times m)$, where n is the amount and m is the number of coin denominations.

Conclusion

Dynamic programming is an essential technique in solving optimization and decision-making problems, especially when subproblems overlap and solving them repeatedly can lead to inefficiencies. By breaking down problems into smaller subproblems and storing the results for future use, dynamic programming significantly optimizes solutions. In this chapter, we covered dynamic programming concepts, explored common problems like the **Knapsack problem, Longest Common Subsequence**, and **Fibonacci sequence**, and discussed real-world applications such as the **Maximum**

Subarray Sum and **Coin Change Problem**. Mastering dynamic programming allows you to approach complex problems more efficiently, and it's a crucial tool for tackling challenging algorithmic problems in coding interviews and real-world systems.

CHAPTER 13

TIME COMPLEXITY AND BIG O NOTATION

Time complexity is a crucial concept in computer science and algorithm design. It helps us understand how the execution time of an algorithm scales with the size of the input. In coding interviews, you'll often be asked to analyze the efficiency of your solutions, not just in terms of correctness but also with respect to time and space resources. In this chapter, we'll explore time complexity, how to calculate it using Big O notation, and provide real-world examples that demonstrate the importance of choosing efficient algorithms.

Introduction to Time Complexity and Why It's Important in Coding Interviews

1. Time Complexity:

- **Time complexity** is a measure of how the runtime of an algorithm grows as the size of the input increases.

It provides a way to quantify the efficiency of an algorithm.

- Understanding time complexity allows developers to make informed decisions about which algorithms and data structures to use based on the size of the input, which is crucial for ensuring scalability and performance, especially when working with large datasets.

2. Why Time Complexity is Important in Coding Interviews:

- In coding interviews, interviewers not only look for correct solutions but also expect you to write **efficient** algorithms that scale well with larger inputs.
- An algorithm that works correctly but takes too long for large inputs is considered inefficient. Understanding time complexity allows you to optimize your code and avoid performance bottlenecks.
- Interviewers often test your ability to improve an initial brute-force solution to a more efficient one by analyzing and optimizing its time complexity.

Analyzing Time and Space Complexity of Algorithms

When analyzing the efficiency of an algorithm, both **time complexity** and **space complexity** should be considered. While time complexity focuses on the amount of time the algorithm takes to complete, space complexity deals with the amount of memory it uses.

1. Time Complexity:

- Time complexity can be calculated by analyzing the number of operations an algorithm performs in relation to the size of the input, usually denoted as nnn.

- For example, if an algorithm iterates through a list of nnn elements, it performs nnn operations, and its time complexity is $O(n)O(n)O(n)$.

- Time complexity is usually expressed using **Big O notation**, which describes the upper bound of an algorithm's growth rate.

2. Space Complexity:

- Space complexity measures the amount of extra memory an algorithm needs to solve a problem, excluding input storage. It accounts for the space used by data structures, recursion stacks, and auxiliary variables.

- For example, if an algorithm stores all its results in an array of size nnn, its space complexity is O(n)O(n)O(n).

How to Calculate Big O Notation for Different Types of Algorithms

Big O notation is used to classify algorithms based on their worst-case performance in terms of the input size. Here are the most common time complexities you'll encounter and how to calculate them:

1. Constant Time O(1)O(1)O(1):

- An algorithm has **constant time complexity** if the number of operations does not depend on the size of the input. It performs the same number of operations regardless of the input size.
- **Example:** Accessing an element in an array by index.

python

```
def get_element(arr, index):
    return arr[index]
```

2. Linear Time O(n)O(n)O(n):

- An algorithm has **linear time complexity** if the number of operations is directly proportional to the size of the input. This means that if the input size doubles, the execution time also doubles.
- **Example:** Iterating through an array of size nnn.

python

```
def print_elements(arr):
    for element in arr:
        print(element)
```

3. Quadratic Time O(n2)O(n^2)O(n2):

- An algorithm has **quadratic time complexity** if the number of operations is proportional to the square of the input size. This often occurs when there are nested loops iterating through the input.
- **Example:** A simple bubble sort implementation, where two nested loops iterate through the array.

python

```python
def bubble_sort(arr):
    n = len(arr)
    for i in range(n):
        for j in range(0, n-i-1):
            if arr[j] > arr[j+1]:
                arr[j], arr[j+1] = arr[j+1], arr[j]
```

4. Logarithmic Time $O(\log n)$ $O(\log n)$ $O(\log n)$:

- An algorithm has **logarithmic time complexity** if the number of operations grows logarithmically with the size of the input. This often happens in algorithms that repeatedly divide the input in half, such as binary search.
- **Example:** Binary search on a sorted array.

python

```python
def binary_search(arr, target):
    left, right = 0, len(arr) - 1
    while left <= right:
        mid = (left + right) // 2
        if arr[mid] == target:
```

151

```
        return mid
    elif arr[mid] < target:
        left = mid + 1
    else:
        right = mid - 1
return -1
```

5. Log-Linear Time O(nlog n)O(n \log n)O(nlogn):

- An algorithm has **log-linear time complexity** if the number of operations is a combination of linear and logarithmic growth. This is common in efficient sorting algorithms like merge sort and quicksort.
- **Example:** Merge sort.

python

```python
def merge_sort(arr):
    if len(arr) > 1:
        mid = len(arr) // 2
        left = arr[:mid]
        right = arr[mid:]
        merge_sort(left)
        merge_sort(right)
        i = j = k = 0
```

```
while i < len(left) and j < len(right):
    if left[i] < right[j]:
        arr[k] = left[i]
        i += 1
    else:
        arr[k] = right[j]
        j += 1
    k += 1
while i < len(left):
    arr[k] = left[i]
    i += 1
    k += 1
while j < len(right):
    arr[k] = right[j]
    j += 1
    k += 1
```

6. Exponential Time O(2n)O(2^n)O(2n):

- An algorithm has **exponential time complexity** if the number of operations doubles with each additional input element. These algorithms are often inefficient and impractical for large inputs.

- **Example:** Solving the **traveling salesman problem** using brute force.

Real-World Examples to Demonstrate the Difference Between Efficient and Inefficient Solutions

Let's take a look at two real-world problems and compare inefficient and efficient solutions using time complexity.

1. Finding the Maximum Subarray Sum:

- **Problem:** Given an array of integers, find the contiguous subarray with the maximum sum.
- **Inefficient Solution (Brute Force):**
    - Using two nested loops to check every possible subarray.
    - **Time Complexity:** $O(n2)O(n^2)O(n2)$

python

```
def max_subarray_sum(arr):
    max_sum = float('-inf')
    for i in range(len(arr)):
        for j in range(i, len(arr)):
            current_sum = sum(arr[i:j+1])
            max_sum = max(max_sum, current_sum)
    return max_sum
```

- **Efficient Solution (Kadane's Algorithm):**
  - Using a single pass through the array to find the maximum subarray sum.
  - **Time Complexity:** $O(n)O(n)O(n)$

python

```python
def max_subarray_sum(arr):
    max_so_far = max_ending_here = arr[0]
    for num in arr[1:]:
        max_ending_here    =    max(num,
max_ending_here + num)
        max_so_far    =    max(max_so_far,
max_ending_here)
    return max_so_far
```

Difference:

- The brute force solution requires $O(n2)O(n^2)O(n2)$ time, which becomes very slow for large inputs.
- The optimized solution using Kadane's algorithm runs in $O(n)O(n)O(n)$ time, making it much more efficient for large arrays.

2. Coin Change Problem:

155

- **Problem:** Given an array of coin denominations and a target amount, find the minimum number of coins required to make that amount.
- **Inefficient Solution (Brute Force):**
  - Trying all possible combinations of coins.
  - **Time Complexity:** $O(2n)O(2^n)O(2n)$ (exponential time)
- **Efficient Solution (Dynamic Programming):**
  - Using dynamic programming to build up the solution iteratively.
  - **Time Complexity:** $O(n \times m)O(n \times m)O(n \times m)$, where nnn is the amount and mmm is the number of coin denominations.

python

```python
def coin_change(coins, amount):
    dp = [float('inf')] * (amount + 1)
    dp[0] = 0
    for coin in coins:
        for i in range(coin, amount + 1):
            dp[i] = min(dp[i], dp[i - coin] + 1)
    return dp[amount] if dp[amount] != float('inf') else -1
```

Difference:

- The brute force solution considers all combinations of coins, leading to an exponential time complexity.
- The dynamic programming solution calculates the minimum coins in polynomial time, significantly improving performance for large amounts.

Conclusion

Understanding time complexity is essential for writing efficient algorithms that scale well with increasing input sizes. In this chapter, we explored the concept of **Big O notation** and how to calculate time and space complexity for different types of algorithms. We also discussed the importance of choosing efficient solutions and demonstrated this with real-world examples like the **maximum subarray sum** and **coin change problem**. By mastering time complexity analysis, you will be better equipped to write algorithms that perform efficiently, even with large datasets, making you a more effective problem solver in coding interviews and real-world applications.

CHAPTER 14

SYSTEM DESIGN INTERVIEWS - AN INTRODUCTION

System design interviews are a crucial part of technical interviews, especially for software engineering roles at top tech companies. These interviews test your ability to design complex systems, ensuring you can architect scalable, reliable, and efficient software. In this chapter, we'll explore what system design interviews are, why they matter, and provide an overview of the system design process. We'll also cover common system design problems, approaches, and real-world examples to give you a deeper understanding of what to expect.

What System Design Interviews Are and Why They Matter

1. System Design Interviews:

- System design interviews assess your ability to design large-scale, distributed systems, and evaluate how well you understand the architectural challenges and trade-offs involved.

- In these interviews, you'll be asked to design a system or a feature from scratch, explaining how you would tackle scalability, performance, reliability, and maintainability challenges.

- The focus is on how you approach the problem rather than a specific coding solution. You'll need to consider factors like load balancing, data storage, fault tolerance, and caching, among others.

2. Why System Design Interviews Matter:

- **Real-World Applications:** System design interviews reflect real-world challenges faced by software engineers when building and maintaining systems at scale.

- **Evaluating Thought Process:** They evaluate your ability to think through complex problems, make decisions, and justify design choices.

- **Key to Scaling Products:** At large tech companies, engineers are often tasked with building systems that can handle millions (or even billions) of users. A solid understanding of system design is critical for creating solutions that are both efficient and scalable.

Overview of the System Design Process

The system design process typically follows several stages, and it's important to understand how to approach each one during a system design interview. Here's an overview of the typical process:

1. Understand the Problem:

- **Clarify Requirements:** Before diving into the design, make sure you fully understand the problem. Ask the interviewer clarifying questions to define both functional and non-functional requirements.
  - ○ **Functional Requirements:** What does the system need to do? What are the main features and capabilities it should provide?
  - ○ **Non-Functional Requirements:** Consider aspects such as scalability, availability, fault tolerance, and performance.

2. High-Level Design:

- **Design at a High Level:** Begin with an abstract design and break down the system into core

160

components (e.g., databases, APIs, services). Focus on major blocks and how they interact.

- **Identify Key Components:** Determine how to divide the system into microservices or modules, and how they will communicate with each other. For example, think about:
  - Data storage and retrieval (e.g., databases, file systems)
  - Communication protocols (e.g., HTTP, gRPC)
  - Caching and load balancing

3. Define Data Models:

- **Data Storage and Modeling:** Decide how to structure and store data. Will you use a relational database, NoSQL, or a hybrid approach? Think about tables, schemas, and indexes for relational databases or document structures for NoSQL databases.

- **Data Consistency and Integrity:** Consider how you will handle consistency, especially in distributed systems. You may need to explain the CAP theorem (Consistency, Availability, Partition Tolerance) and decide which aspects are most important for your design.

161

4. Handle Scalability and Reliability:

- **Scalability:** Think about how the system will scale with increasing load. Consider horizontal scaling (adding more machines) vs. vertical scaling (adding resources to a single machine).
- **Reliability:** Plan for fault tolerance by considering redundancy, failover mechanisms, and backup strategies. Think about how to handle failure scenarios, such as network failures or server crashes.

5. Performance Optimization:

- **Caching:** Think about caching strategies to improve performance. What data should be cached, and where should the cache be stored (e.g., in-memory cache, CDN)?
- **Load Balancing:** Consider load balancing strategies to distribute traffic evenly across servers.
- **Latency and Throughput:** Evaluate the system's latency and throughput and how to minimize bottlenecks.

6. Conclusion and Trade-offs:

- **Explain Trade-offs:** System design often involves trade-offs between scalability, consistency, cost, and complexity. Be prepared to explain why you chose one approach over another.

- **Provide Next Steps:** Once the initial design is complete, consider adding features like monitoring, logging, and security measures.

Common System Design Problems and Approaches

Here are some common types of system design problems you might encounter, along with general approaches to solving them:

1. Design a URL Shortener:

- **Problem:** Design a system like bit.ly that shortens long URLs to a unique identifier and allows redirection to the original URL.

- **Approach:**
    - **High-Level Design:** Implement a database to store the mapping of short URLs to original URLs. Use a hash function or an auto-increment ID to generate short URLs.

- o **Scalability:** Use a distributed database or sharding for scalability. Consider caching popular URLs to reduce database load.
- o **Redirection:** Implement a fast lookup system for redirecting short URLs to their original counterparts.

2. Design a Social Media Feed:

- **Problem:** Design a system like Facebook or Twitter that displays a user's feed, with posts from friends or followed users.
- **Approach:**
  - o **High-Level Design:** Create an entity for users, posts, and follows. Users can follow other users, and each post is associated with a user. The feed is generated by fetching posts from users a person follows.
  - o **Scalability:** Use a distributed cache to store frequently accessed posts. Implement paging and lazy loading for large feeds.
  - o **Data Modeling:** Use a NoSQL database (e.g., MongoDB) to store posts and a relational database for user information.

3. Design an Online Auction System:

- **Problem:** Design a system that allows users to place bids on items and track the highest bid in real-time.
- **Approach:**
  - **High-Level Design:** Use a message queue to handle real-time bid updates. Store auction items and bids in a database.
  - **Concurrency:** Handle bid conflicts using optimistic locking or a distributed lock to prevent bid races.
  - **Scalability:** Use partitioning (sharding) to handle large volumes of bids and ensure low-latency updates.

Real-World Examples of System Design Problems

Let's look at some real-world examples where system design principles are applied:

1. Design a Ride-Sharing System (e.g., Uber):

- **Problem:** Design a system that matches passengers with available drivers in real-time, calculates fares, and manages ride statuses.

- **Approach:**
  - **High-Level Design:** Use GPS data to track drivers and passengers. Create an algorithm to match available drivers to passengers based on location. Use a message queue for real-time updates.
  - **Scalability:** Use a distributed database to store user profiles, ride history, and payment details.
  - **Performance:** Cache driver availability and location data for quick matching.

2. Design a Distributed File Storage System (e.g., Google Drive):

- **Problem:** Design a system that allows users to upload, store, and share large files across devices.
- **Approach:**
  - **High-Level Design:** Implement file storage using a distributed file system, such as HDFS or a cloud-based object storage service. Use hashing to organize and locate files.
  - **Redundancy:** Ensure fault tolerance with data replication. Use sharding to scale the system horizontally.

   o **Security:** Implement access control for file sharing, and encrypt sensitive data.

3. Design an E-commerce Website (e.g., Amazon):

- **Problem:** Design an e-commerce system that handles product catalog management, user accounts, orders, and payments.
- **Approach:**
  - o **High-Level Design:** Use a relational database to manage product catalogs, user accounts, and orders. Implement a shopping cart system with session management.
  - o **Scalability:** Implement a microservices architecture to scale individual components like the catalog and payment system independently.
  - o **Security:** Ensure user privacy and data protection through encryption and secure payment gateways.

Conclusion

System design interviews are essential in assessing your ability to architect scalable and reliable systems. By understanding the process of system design, including how to break down a problem into smaller components, make trade-offs, and optimize for scalability and reliability, you can confidently tackle system design questions in interviews. In this chapter, we've explored common system design problems, discussed approaches to solving them, and looked at real-world examples where system design principles are applied. Mastering system design will prepare you to handle complex challenges in software engineering and ensure you can build systems that meet the demands of users and the business.

CHAPTER 15

DESIGNING SCALABLE SYSTEMS

Scalability is one of the most important aspects of modern system design. As the demands on systems grow, it is crucial to ensure that the architecture can handle increasing loads without compromising performance or reliability. Designing scalable systems involves understanding key concepts like load balancing, sharding, and replication. In this chapter, we'll explore these concepts and discuss how to design scalable systems and services, using real-world examples such as designing a URL shortener and a social media platform.

Key Concepts in Scalability: Load Balancing, Sharding, and Replication

1. Load Balancing:

- **Definition:** Load balancing is the process of distributing incoming network traffic or computational tasks across multiple servers to ensure that no single server is overwhelmed. The goal is to ensure high availability and reliability by preventing any one server from becoming a bottleneck.

- **How it Works:** Load balancers monitor the health and availability of servers and route requests to the least-loaded or most responsive servers. This helps evenly distribute traffic and prevent server downtime.

- **Types of Load Balancers:**
  - **Hardware Load Balancers:** Specialized physical devices that distribute network traffic across multiple servers.
  - **Software Load Balancers:** Software solutions like **HAProxy**, **Nginx**, or cloud-native solutions (e.g., AWS Elastic Load Balancing) that distribute traffic at the application layer.

- **Real-World Example:** In an e-commerce system, load balancers ensure that user requests are routed to available web servers, preventing server overload during high traffic periods (e.g., Black Friday sales).

2. Sharding:

- **Definition:** Sharding is the practice of breaking up large datasets into smaller, manageable pieces (called **shards**) and distributing them across multiple servers. This approach is used to horizontally scale databases by partitioning data to improve performance and storage capacity.

- **How it Works:** Each shard holds a subset of the data, and the system uses a **shard key** to determine how data is distributed. Shards can be based on customer IDs, geographic locations, or other criteria.

- **Types of Sharding:**
  - **Horizontal Sharding:** Data is split into different rows or entries and distributed across multiple machines (e.g., users with IDs 1–100 go to one shard, and users with IDs 101–200 go to another).
  - **Vertical Sharding:** Different pieces of data (e.g., user data, transaction data) are stored on separate servers.

- **Real-World Example:** In a social media platform, sharding can be used to store user data based on geographic regions or user ID ranges. This ensures that the system can handle millions of users without hitting the performance limits of a single database.

3. Replication:

- **Definition:** Replication is the process of creating copies of data across multiple servers. It ensures that data is highly available and durable, even in the case of server failure.

- **How it Works:** Data is replicated across several nodes in the system. Typically, there are **master** (primary) nodes that handle writes and **replica** (secondary) nodes that handle reads. In some configurations, writes can also be distributed across replicas to increase write throughput.

- **Types of Replication:**
    - ○ **Master-Slave Replication:** A master node handles write operations, while slave nodes serve read requests.
    - ○ **Multi-Master Replication:** Multiple nodes handle both reads and writes, and changes are synchronized across all nodes.
    - ○ **Eventual Consistency:** In some distributed systems, updates to replicas may not be immediate, but the system guarantees that all replicas will eventually become consistent.

- **Real-World Example:** In a global-scale application like a social media platform, replication ensures that users can access their data quickly regardless of their

172

geographic location, reducing latency by serving data from nearby replicas.

How to Design Scalable Systems and Services

Designing scalable systems involves carefully considering how each component interacts with others to ensure that the system can handle increased loads as demand grows. Here are some general principles and approaches to designing scalable systems:

1. Identify the Scaling Requirements:

- **Vertical Scaling (Scaling Up):** Adding more resources (CPU, memory, etc.) to a single server. This can work for smaller applications but is often limited by the capacity of the hardware.
- **Horizontal Scaling (Scaling Out):** Adding more servers to distribute the load. This is the preferred method for scaling large-scale systems, as it allows for flexibility and redundancy.

2. Decouple Components Using Microservices:

- Break down the system into smaller, independent services (microservices) that can be scaled individually. This avoids the single monolithic application that may become a bottleneck.
- Each microservice should focus on a specific responsibility (e.g., user authentication, payment processing) and communicate with other services through APIs.

3. Use Distributed Caching:

- Implement caching layers to reduce the load on databases and improve response times. Distributed caches (like **Redis** or **Memcached**) store frequently accessed data in memory to quickly serve repeated requests.

4. Optimize Data Access:

- Use **indexing, denormalization**, and **read replicas** to speed up database queries.
- For large datasets, consider using a **NoSQL database** (e.g., **Cassandra**, **MongoDB**) that can scale horizontally and handle unstructured data.

5. Implement Fault Tolerance:

- Design the system to handle failures gracefully. Use **replication** to ensure data availability and implement **health checks** to monitor the status of components.

- Use **retry logic** and **circuit breakers** to handle temporary failures and prevent cascading system failures.

6. Consider Latency and Consistency:

- Balance between **latency** (response time) and **consistency** (accuracy of data). Some systems prioritize speed (eventual consistency) over consistency, while others may require strict consistency (strong consistency).

- Use techniques like **sharding** and **replication** to reduce latency and improve availability.

Real-World Examples of Scalable System Designs

Let's look at two real-world examples to demonstrate how scalability principles are applied:

1. Designing a URL Shortener:

- **Problem:** A system like Bit.ly that shortens long URLs to a unique identifier and allows redirection to the original URL.
- **High-Level Design:**
    - Use a **database** to store the mapping of short URLs to original URLs.
    - Use a **hash function** or auto-incrementing IDs to generate unique short URLs.
    - **Sharding:** As the number of users and URLs grows, distribute the URL data across multiple servers using sharding techniques based on user ID or URL prefixes.
    - **Replication:** Replicate the URL mapping data across multiple servers to ensure high availability and reduce latency in accessing the URL mappings.
    - **Load Balancing:** Distribute user requests across multiple servers to handle high traffic volumes.
- **Scalability:** Implement a distributed cache like **Redis** to store frequently accessed URLs and reduce database load.

2. Designing a Social Media Platform:

- **Problem:** Design a system that allows users to post content, interact with other users, and follow friends or other accounts.

- **High-Level Design:**
  - Use a **relational database** for user accounts and relationships, and a **NoSQL database** for storing posts and interactions.

  - **Sharding:** Partition user data based on geographical regions or user IDs to balance the load across multiple servers.

  - **Replication:** Use **master-slave replication** to store user profiles on master nodes and use replicas to handle read requests from different geographical regions.

  - **Caching:** Use **CDNs** to cache media files and **Redis** for caching popular posts or feeds to speed up response times.

  - **Load Balancing:** Distribute traffic evenly across servers, ensuring that no single server is overwhelmed during high-traffic periods (e.g., viral posts).

- **Scalability:** Use **microservices architecture** to scale independent services like authentication, media uploads, and user feeds separately.

Conclusion

Designing scalable systems is a crucial skill for building systems that can handle growing user bases and increasing demands. Key concepts like **load balancing, sharding**, and **replication** are essential for achieving scalability, performance, and fault tolerance. In this chapter, we've explored the principles of scalable system design and provided real-world examples such as designing a **URL shortener** and a **social media platform**. By understanding and applying these principles, you can build systems that scale efficiently and meet the needs of millions or even billions of users.

CHAPTER 16

DATABASES AND DATA STORAGE

Databases are the backbone of most modern applications, providing the necessary storage and retrieval mechanisms for structured and unstructured data. Understanding the different types of databases and when to use them is essential for building efficient, scalable systems. In this chapter, we will explore the differences between **relational databases** and **NoSQL databases**, how to choose the right database for your system, and the best practices for designing database schemas for system design problems. We will also discuss real-world examples like designing a library system and implementing a cache system.

Relational Databases vs. NoSQL Databases

1. Relational Databases:

- **Definition:** Relational databases store data in structured tables that are related to each other. Each

179

table consists of rows (records) and columns (attributes), and the relationships between tables are established using **foreign keys**.

- **Characteristics:**
  - **ACID Properties:** Relational databases ensure **Atomicity**, **Consistency**, **Isolation**, and **Durability** for transactions, making them suitable for applications where data consistency is critical.
  - **Structured Data:** The schema is predefined, and data must follow a rigid structure, typically defined using SQL (Structured Query Language).
  - **Examples:** MySQL, PostgreSQL, Microsoft SQL Server, Oracle.

- **Use Cases:**
  - Financial systems (banking transactions), inventory management, and any application that requires complex queries and transactions with strong consistency guarantees.

2. NoSQL Databases:

- **Definition:** NoSQL databases are a class of databases designed to handle unstructured or semi-structured data that doesn't fit well into tables. These databases are more flexible than relational databases and can store large volumes of diverse data types.

- **Types of NoSQL Databases:**
  - **Document-Oriented:** Stores data in the form of documents, typically in JSON or BSON format. Examples: MongoDB, CouchDB.

  - **Key-Value Stores:** Stores data as key-value pairs, ideal for caching and session storage. Examples: Redis, DynamoDB.

  - **Column-Family Stores:** Stores data in columns rather than rows, useful for large-scale analytical applications. Examples: Cassandra, HBase.

  - **Graph Databases:** Used for data with complex relationships, such as social networks. Examples: Neo4j, Amazon Neptune.

- **Characteristics:**
  - **Flexible Schema:** NoSQL databases generally allow you to store data without a

181

predefined schema, making them suitable for rapidly evolving applications.

- o **Scalability:** NoSQL databases are designed for horizontal scaling and can handle large volumes of data and high-velocity reads/writes.

- o **Eventual Consistency:** Many NoSQL databases prioritize availability and partition tolerance over consistency (according to the **CAP theorem**).

- **Use Cases:**

  - o Real-time analytics, big data applications, social media platforms, and applications with rapidly changing data or large volumes of semi-structured data.

How to Choose the Right Database for Your System

When selecting a database for your system, consider the following factors to determine whether a **relational** or **NoSQL** database is the right fit:

1. Data Structure:

- If your data is **highly structured** with complex relationships (e.g., transactional data, financial records), a **relational database** is likely the better choice.

- If your data is **semi-structured or unstructured** (e.g., JSON documents, logs, social media data), a **NoSQL database** may offer more flexibility.

2. Scalability Requirements:

- **Relational Databases:** While they can be scaled vertically (adding more resources to a single machine), they are typically less suited for **horizontal scaling** (scaling across multiple machines).

- **NoSQL Databases:** Designed for **horizontal scaling**, they are well-suited for systems that require high availability and the ability to handle large volumes of data spread across many servers.

3. Consistency vs. Availability:

- **Relational Databases:** Prioritize **strong consistency** and are ideal for applications where

183

maintaining data integrity and ensuring ACID properties are crucial.

- **NoSQL Databases:** Typically offer **eventual consistency** and are better suited for applications that require high availability and partition tolerance, like social networks or real-time data processing.

4. Transaction Support:

- If your application requires **complex transactions** (e.g., bank transfers), **relational databases** are the better choice, as they support ACID transactions.
- For applications that don't need strong transactional guarantees (e.g., caching or session management), **NoSQL databases** can be a better fit.

5. Query Complexity:

- **Relational Databases:** If your application requires **complex joins**, aggregations, and transactions, relational databases are better suited because of their powerful SQL query capabilities.
- **NoSQL Databases:** If your application requires **simple lookups**, and you need high-performance

reads/writes, NoSQL databases like **Redis** or **Cassandra** can be more efficient.

Designing Database Schemas for System Design Problems

Designing an effective database schema is crucial for ensuring that the system is scalable, maintainable, and performant. Here are key considerations for designing database schemas:

1. Normalize the Schema (For Relational Databases):

- **Normalization** ensures that data is stored efficiently without redundancy, which reduces the chances of anomalies.
- It involves organizing tables into smaller, more manageable units (e.g., dividing large tables into smaller related tables).
- Use **foreign keys** to maintain relationships between tables.

Example:

- **Library System:** The schema could include tables like Books, Authors, Customers, and Transactions,

185

with foreign keys linking Books to Authors and Customers to Transactions.

2. Denormalization (For NoSQL Databases):

- In **NoSQL databases**, denormalization is often used, where redundant data is stored for faster reads.
- While this increases data duplication, it can reduce the complexity of joins and improve performance in read-heavy applications.

Example:

- **Social Media Platform:** A denormalized schema could store user posts with embedded user profiles, comments, and likes directly within each post document, avoiding the need for joins.

3. Indexing:

- **Indexes** are essential for optimizing query performance, especially for searching or retrieving large datasets.
- Use indexing to speed up searches based on frequently queried fields, such as user_id or post_id.

4. Partitioning (Sharding) Data:

- Partition your data across multiple tables or databases to improve performance and scalability.
- For example, in a large-scale **e-commerce platform**, you could shard the Orders table by customer region, ensuring that no single database holds too much data.

Real-World Examples

Let's look at how database design principles are applied in real-world scenarios:

1. Designing a Library System:

- **Problem:** A library system needs to manage books, customers, transactions, and inventory.
- **Database Design (Relational Database):**
  - ○ **Tables:**
    - ▪ Books (book_id, title, author_id, publication_year, genre)
    - ▪ Authors (author_id, name)
    - ▪ Customers (customer_id, name, address, phone_number)

187

- Transactions (transaction_id, customer_id, book_id, issue_date, return_date)
  - **Relationships:**
    - Books and Authors are linked by author_id.
    - Transactions and Books are linked by book_id, and Transactions and Customers are linked by customer_id.
  - **Indexing:** Index the book_id, customer_id, and issue_date for efficient searching and transaction history retrieval.

Real-World Considerations:

- To scale, the system could be partitioned by region, with each regional database handling the books and customers in that region.
- **Replication** can be used for high availability, ensuring that users can access book information even if one server fails.

2. Implementing a Cache System:

- **Problem:** A website needs to quickly retrieve frequently accessed data, like user session information, without querying the database every time.

- **Database Design (NoSQL Database):**
  - o Use a **key-value store** like **Redis** or **Memcached** to cache frequently accessed data.
  - o **Keys:** Cache keys could be user session IDs or product IDs, with the corresponding data (user information or product details) stored as the value.
  - o **Expiration:** Cache entries should have an expiration time (TTL) to ensure that outdated data is eventually purged from the cache.

Real-World Considerations:

- The cache system helps reduce database load by providing fast, low-latency access to frequently accessed data.

- To scale, use **horizontal scaling** of the cache servers to handle high volumes of requests.

Conclusion

Databases are at the heart of many systems, and understanding how to choose the right database, design schemas, and implement data storage strategies is crucial for building scalable and efficient systems. In this chapter, we explored the differences between **relational** and **NoSQL databases**, how to choose the right database for a given system, and the best practices for designing database schemas. We also provided real-world examples like designing a **library system** and implementing a **cache system**, highlighting the application of these principles. By mastering database design and storage strategies, you will be equipped to build systems that handle large volumes of data efficiently and scale with growing demands.

CHAPTER 17

DISTRIBUTED SYSTEMS - COMMUNICATION AND COORDINATION

Distributed systems are complex architectures where components are spread across multiple machines, often in different geographic locations, but work together as a single unified system. In such systems, ensuring reliable communication, fault tolerance, and scalability is crucial. This chapter will explore the core principles of distributed systems, including the **CAP theorem**, techniques for building reliable and fault-tolerant systems, and real-world examples like designing a file storage system and building a messaging service.

Principles of Distributed Systems: Consistency, Availability, and Partition Tolerance (CAP Theorem)

The **CAP theorem**, introduced by computer scientist Eric Brewer, describes the fundamental trade-offs that must be made when designing distributed systems. The theorem states that a distributed system can achieve at most two out of the three following goals:

- **Consistency (C):** Every read operation on the system will return the most recent write. In other words, all nodes in the system have the same data at the same time. When a client reads from the system, it is guaranteed to see the most recent state of the data.

- **Availability (A):** Every request (read or write) to the system will receive a response, even if some of the nodes are unavailable. The system ensures that the client will always get a response, though it may not always be the most up-to-date version of the data.

- **Partition Tolerance (P):** The system can continue to operate correctly even if network partitions (communication failures) occur between nodes. This is critical for large-scale systems that must operate across unreliable networks.

CAP Theorem and Trade-offs:

- A system can only guarantee two of these three properties at the same time. For example:

- **CA (Consistency and Availability)** systems sacrifice partition tolerance. They can't continue to function correctly when network failures occur but will ensure that every node has the same data and always responds to requests.

- **CP (Consistency and Partition Tolerance)** systems ensure that all nodes remain consistent and operational even when network partitions occur, but may sacrifice availability when some nodes are unable to respond.

- **AP (Availability and Partition Tolerance)** systems ensure that the system remains available and operational even with network partitions, but may return stale data or inconsistent results.

The CAP theorem emphasizes that in distributed systems, you must choose between consistency, availability, and partition tolerance depending on the specific requirements of the application.

Techniques for Building Reliable and Fault-Tolerant Systems

Building reliable and fault-tolerant distributed systems involves several key strategies and techniques:

1. Redundancy and Replication:

- **Redundancy** ensures that data is stored in multiple places (e.g., replicated across several nodes). This protects the system from failures by ensuring that if one node fails, data can still be retrieved from another node.

- **Replication Strategies:**
  - **Master-Slave Replication:** One node (master) handles all write operations, and one or more nodes (slaves) replicate the data for read operations.
  - **Multi-Master Replication:** All nodes can handle read and write operations, and the system ensures data consistency across all nodes.

2. Consensus Algorithms:

- **Consensus** algorithms are used in distributed systems to ensure that all nodes agree on the current state of the system, especially when network failures or crashes occur. These algorithms ensure that the system remains in a consistent state even in the presence of partial failures.

- **Examples of Consensus Algorithms:**
  - **Paxos:** A well-known algorithm used to achieve consensus in distributed systems, often used in systems like **Google Chubby** and **Apache Zookeeper**.
  - **Raft:** A more recent consensus algorithm that is easier to understand than Paxos and is used in systems like **etcd** and **Consul**.

3. Data Partitioning (Sharding):

- **Sharding** involves dividing the data into smaller pieces called "shards" and distributing them across multiple machines or nodes. This helps to scale the system horizontally, making it easier to handle large amounts of data and traffic.

- Each shard contains a subset of the data, and systems use techniques like consistent hashing to determine where data should be placed and retrieved.

195

4. Fault Detection and Recovery:

- **Fault tolerance** is essential in distributed systems. The system should be able to detect when a node is down or unreachable and automatically reroute requests to healthy nodes.
- Techniques like **heartbeat messages** or **failure detectors** are used to monitor node health. If a failure is detected, the system can initiate a **failover** process to another replica or node to maintain service availability.

5. Eventual Consistency:

- In some distributed systems, **eventual consistency** is used instead of strict consistency. This means that, while data might be inconsistent across nodes temporarily, the system guarantees that all nodes will eventually converge to the same state once the system stabilizes.
- **Eventual consistency** is often used in systems like **Cassandra** and **Amazon DynamoDB**, where availability and partition tolerance are prioritized over strict consistency.

Real-World Examples of Distributed Systems

1. Designing a File Storage System:

Problem: Design a distributed file storage system that can store and retrieve files reliably, ensuring high availability and fault tolerance across multiple data centers.

High-Level Design:

- **Data Storage:** Use a **distributed file system** like **HDFS (Hadoop Distributed File System)** or **Amazon S3**. Data is split into smaller blocks and distributed across multiple nodes.

- **Replication:** To ensure fault tolerance, use **replication** where each file block is copied to multiple nodes. This ensures data availability even if one node fails.

- **Metadata Management:** Use a **metadata server** to track the location of file blocks across the cluster. Systems like **HDFS NameNode** or **Amazon S3's metadata service** track file locations.

- **Sharding:** Store files in different nodes based on their size or type, making it easier to scale the system horizontally as the volume of data grows.

- **Load Balancing:** Use a **load balancer** to distribute requests to different file storage nodes to ensure the system can handle a large number of read/write requests simultaneously.

- **Eventual Consistency:** Implement **eventual consistency** for file replication, allowing data to be consistent across nodes after a period of time.

Scalability: The system can be scaled by adding more nodes to store additional data and by replicating files across multiple regions to ensure low-latency access.

---

2. Building a Messaging Service:

Problem: Design a messaging service like **WhatsApp** or **Slack**, which needs to support sending and receiving messages in real-time, storing messages, and handling millions of active users simultaneously.

High-Level Design:

- **Messaging Protocol:** Use a real-time messaging protocol like **WebSockets** or **MQTT** for bidirectional communication between clients and servers.

- **Message Queue:** Implement a **message queue** system like **Kafka** or **RabbitMQ** to handle message delivery between users. These systems can handle high-throughput messaging and allow for retry mechanisms in case of failure.

- **Sharding:** Distribute messages across multiple servers using **sharding** based on user IDs or message timestamps. This helps distribute the load and ensures horizontal scalability.

- **Replication:** Use **replication** to ensure that messages are available even if one of the messaging servers fails. Multiple copies of message data can be stored in different geographic regions to ensure high availability and low-latency access.

- **Consistency:** Implement **eventual consistency** for delivering messages, as messages might be delayed due to network partitions or server failures, but the system guarantees that they will be delivered eventually.

- **Fault Tolerance:** Use **failover mechanisms** and **health checks** to monitor server statuses. If one server goes down, traffic is automatically routed to another server to maintain availability.

- **Notification System:** Use a **push notification system** to notify users of new messages even when they are not actively using the app.

Scalability: The system can scale by adding more message queues, replication nodes, and web servers to handle the increased load during peak times (e.g., holidays or special events).

Conclusion

Distributed systems are essential for building modern, large-scale applications that require high availability, fault tolerance, and scalability. The **CAP theorem** helps guide system design by emphasizing the trade-offs between consistency, availability, and partition tolerance. Techniques such as **load balancing, sharding**, and **replication** are critical for building reliable and scalable distributed systems. In this chapter, we explored how to design scalable systems using real-world examples, including designing a **file storage system** and building a **messaging service**. By mastering these principles and techniques, you'll be equipped to design robust, scalable systems that can handle the demands of modern applications.

CHAPTER 18

DESIGNING APIS AND MICROSERVICES

APIs (Application Programming Interfaces) and microservices are foundational concepts in modern software architecture. They enable systems to be modular, flexible, and scalable, facilitating communication and integration between different parts of an application or with external systems. In this chapter, we will explore what APIs and microservices are, why they are important, and the key principles for designing robust and scalable APIs. We will also provide real-world examples like designing **RESTful APIs** and building **microservices** for an e-commerce platform.

What are APIs and Microservices, and Why Are They Important?

1. APIs (Application Programming Interfaces):

- **Definition:** An API is a set of rules that allows one piece of software or system to communicate with another. APIs define the methods and data formats that applications can use to request and exchange data, enabling interoperability between different software components.

- **Types of APIs:**
  - **RESTful APIs:** These APIs adhere to the principles of REST (Representational State Transfer) and use HTTP methods (GET, POST, PUT, DELETE) to interact with resources.
  - **SOAP APIs:** A more rigid, XML-based protocol used for message exchange in older systems.
  - **GraphQL APIs:** A flexible query language for APIs, allowing clients to request exactly the data they need.
  - **WebSocket APIs:** Used for real-time, full-duplex communication between clients and servers.

- **Importance of APIs:**
  - **Interoperability:** APIs enable different systems and applications to communicate

with each other, regardless of their underlying technology.

- o **Extensibility:** APIs allow developers to extend existing systems with new functionality without modifying the underlying codebase.

- o **Third-Party Integrations:** APIs provide a standardized way for external services to interact with your system, enabling integrations with other platforms (e.g., payment gateways, third-party data services).

2. Microservices:

- **Definition:** Microservices is an architectural style where an application is composed of loosely coupled, independently deployable services, each focused on a specific business functionality. These services communicate with each other using APIs.

- **Characteristics of Microservices:**
  - o **Single Responsibility:** Each microservice is designed to perform one specific function or business capability.

- o **Independent Deployability:** Microservices can be developed, deployed, and scaled independently.
- o **Technology Agnostic:** Different microservices can be built using different technologies or programming languages, based on the requirements.

- **Importance of Microservices:**
  - o **Scalability:** Microservices enable horizontal scaling by allowing independent scaling of specific services based on load.
  - o **Resilience:** If one microservice fails, it does not necessarily bring down the entire system, improving the overall resilience of the application.
  - o **Faster Development and Deployment:** Since microservices are independent, development teams can work on different services simultaneously, speeding up feature development and deployment.
  - o **Flexibility in Technology Choices:** Microservices can use different databases, programming languages, and frameworks

suited to the service's needs, enhancing flexibility and optimization.

Principles for Designing Robust and Scalable APIs

Designing APIs that are both **robust** and **scalable** is crucial for building systems that can handle high volumes of traffic while remaining maintainable. Here are the key principles to follow:

1. Follow RESTful Design Principles (For REST APIs):

- **Statelessness:** Each API request should contain all the information necessary to process the request, as the server should not store any client context between requests.
- **Use HTTP Methods Correctly:**
  - **GET:** Retrieve data.
  - **POST:** Create data.
  - **PUT:** Update data.
  - **DELETE:** Remove data.
- **Use Meaningful and Consistent Endpoints:** Endpoint URLs should be intuitive and describe the resource being accessed. For example:

- o GET /users (retrieves a list of users)

- o POST /users (creates a new user)

- o GET /users/{id} (retrieves a specific user by ID)

- o PUT /users/{id} (updates a specific user by ID)

- o DELETE /users/{id} (deletes a specific user by ID)

- **Use Query Parameters for Filtering, Sorting, and Pagination:** Enable clients to filter results (e.g., GET /users?status=active), sort data (e.g., GET /users?sort=age), and paginate large datasets (e.g., GET /users?page=2&limit=50).

2. Design for Scalability and Performance:

- **Rate Limiting:** Prevent abuse and overload by limiting the number of requests a client can make to the API within a given period.

- **Caching:** Cache frequently accessed data to reduce load on the server and improve response times. Use HTTP caching headers or a dedicated caching layer (e.g., **Redis**).

- **Asynchronous Processing:** For long-running tasks, consider using **asynchronous processing** (e.g., queues, background jobs) to avoid blocking the API response.

- **Load Balancing:** Distribute traffic across multiple API instances to ensure high availability and even load distribution.

3. Security and Authentication:

- **Use OAuth or JWT (JSON Web Tokens):** Secure your APIs by implementing authentication and authorization mechanisms such as OAuth or JWT to control access.

- **Encrypt Sensitive Data:** Use **HTTPS** to encrypt data transmitted between the client and the server, ensuring data privacy and integrity.

- **API Rate Limiting and Throttling:** Implement security features like rate limiting and throttling to prevent DDoS attacks and excessive load on your servers.

4. Versioning:

- **Version Your API:** As your API evolves, it's important to maintain backward compatibility. Versioning helps avoid breaking changes for existing clients. Use versioning in the URL (e.g., /v1/users, /v2/users) or in the headers.

5. Error Handling and Logging:

- **Clear Error Messages:** Provide clear and consistent error messages with HTTP status codes (e.g., 400 Bad Request, 404 Not Found, 500 Internal Server Error) to help developers understand and fix issues quickly.
- **Logging and Monitoring:** Implement logging and monitoring to track API usage, performance, and errors, enabling you to proactively address potential issues.

Real-World Examples

1. Designing RESTful APIs:

Problem: You need to design a **RESTful API** for a task management application that allows users to create, update, delete, and retrieve tasks.

API Design:

- **End Points:**
  - GET /tasks: Retrieves all tasks.
  - POST /tasks: Creates a new task.
  - GET /tasks/{id}: Retrieves a specific task by ID.
  - PUT /tasks/{id}: Updates a task by ID.
  - DELETE /tasks/{id}: Deletes a task by ID.

Considerations:

- **Filtering and Sorting:** Allow users to filter tasks by status (e.g., GET /tasks?status=completed) and sort by due date (e.g., GET /tasks?sort=due_date).
- **Pagination:** Implement pagination for task lists, as there may be thousands of tasks in the system (e.g., GET /tasks?page=2&limit=50).
- **Authentication:** Use **JWT** for authentication to ensure only authorized users can perform actions on tasks.

2. Building Microservices for an E-commerce Platform:

Problem: You need to build a microservices-based e-commerce platform where services like **product**

management, order processing, and **user authentication** are decoupled into independent services.

Microservices Design:

- **Services:**
    - **Product Service:** Manages product catalogs (adding, updating, and deleting products).
    - **Order Service:** Manages customer orders, order status, and payment processing.
    - **User Service:** Handles user registration, login, and account management.
- **API Gateway:** Use an **API Gateway** to provide a single entry point to access all microservices. The gateway routes incoming requests to the appropriate service and handles concerns like authentication and rate limiting.

Key Considerations:

- **Inter-Service Communication:** Services communicate with each other using lightweight protocols like **REST** or **gRPC**. For example, the **Order Service** may call the **Product Service** to check stock availability.

211

- **Data Management:** Use separate databases for each microservice to avoid tight coupling. For example, the **Product Service** can use a **NoSQL** database, while the **Order Service** uses a **relational database**.
- **Service Discovery:** Use a service discovery tool (e.g., **Consul**, **Eureka**) to allow services to discover and communicate with each other dynamically, especially in a scalable microservices architecture.

Conclusion

APIs and microservices are essential components of modern software systems, providing modularity, scalability, and flexibility. Designing robust and scalable APIs requires a focus on usability, performance, security, and versioning, while microservices enable independent scaling and development of system components. In this chapter, we explored how to design **RESTful APIs** and build **microservices** for complex systems, such as an **e-commerce platform**. By applying best practices in API design and microservice architecture, you can create systems that are scalable, maintainable, and resilient to change.

CHAPTER 19

LOAD BALANCING AND CACHING

In high-traffic, distributed systems, achieving both scalability and low latency is crucial. **Load balancing** and **caching** are two essential techniques that help ensure systems can handle large amounts of traffic efficiently while reducing response times. In this chapter, we will explore the key concepts of **load balancing** and **caching**, how they improve system performance, and their role in building scalable systems. Additionally, we will look at real-world examples like designing a **Content Delivery Network (CDN)** and implementing caching for a **news website**.

Introduction to Load Balancing and How to Distribute Traffic Across Servers

1. What is Load Balancing?

- **Load balancing** is the process of distributing incoming network traffic or computational tasks

213

across multiple servers to ensure that no single server is overwhelmed. This helps to ensure high availability, reliability, and performance of your system.

- The goal of load balancing is to optimize resource utilization, minimize response time, and ensure that the system can scale to handle a growing number of requests without overloading any individual server.

2. Types of Load Balancing:

- **Layer 4 (TCP/UDP) Load Balancing:** Operates at the transport layer and handles routing traffic based on IP addresses and ports. It is faster but less granular in terms of traffic distribution.

- **Layer 7 (Application) Load Balancing:** Operates at the application layer and is more flexible, allowing traffic distribution based on HTTP headers, cookies, and other application-level data. It can handle more complex routing decisions like load balancing based on URL paths or request types (e.g., GET vs POST).

3. Load Balancing Algorithms:

- **Round Robin:** Requests are distributed sequentially across all available servers in a circular manner. This is simple but may not account for the individual server load or performance.

- **Least Connections:** Traffic is routed to the server with the fewest active connections. This approach ensures that servers are not overloaded with too many concurrent requests.

- **Weighted Round Robin:** A more advanced version of round-robin that assigns a weight to each server based on its capacity. Servers with higher weights receive more traffic.

- **IP Hashing:** The client's IP address is used to determine which server will handle the request. This can be useful for session persistence (sticky sessions).

4. Benefits of Load Balancing:

- **Scalability:** Enables horizontal scaling by adding more servers to handle increased traffic.

- **Fault Tolerance:** If one server fails, the load balancer can route traffic to other healthy servers, ensuring system availability.

- **Improved Performance:** By distributing traffic evenly, load balancers prevent individual servers from becoming bottlenecks, ensuring faster response times.

Techniques for Implementing Caching and Reducing System Latency

1. What is Caching?

- **Caching** involves storing frequently accessed data in a temporary storage location (cache) to reduce the time it takes to retrieve that data in the future. The idea is to serve data from the cache rather than querying a database or performing complex computations repeatedly.
- Caching is especially useful for read-heavy applications where certain data does not change frequently, allowing it to be reused for multiple requests.

2. Types of Caching:

- **In-Memory Caching:** Stores data in the system's RAM for ultra-fast retrieval. Common in-memory caching solutions include **Redis** and **Memcached**.

- **Distributed Caching:** Involves using a caching layer that spans multiple nodes, often across data centers, to store and serve data across a distributed system. Solutions like **Redis Cluster** and **Amazon ElastiCache** can be used to manage distributed caches.

- **Content Delivery Networks (CDNs):** A specialized form of caching that caches static content (images, videos, scripts) at edge locations close to the end-users, improving load times for global audiences.

- **Database Caching:** Caching query results or partial query results to reduce the load on the database and improve response times for frequently accessed data.

3. Cache Strategies:

- **Cache-Aside (Lazy Loading):** The application checks the cache for data first. If the data isn't found, it fetches the data from the underlying data store and then places it in the cache.

- **Write-Through Caching:** Data is written to both the cache and the underlying data store at the same time. This ensures that the cache is always up-to-date.

- **Time-Based Expiration (TTL):** Cached data is automatically invalidated after a certain period, ensuring that stale data is not served to clients.

- **Cache Eviction Policies:** When the cache reaches its storage limit, data that's least likely to be used next (Least Recently Used - LRU) or least important can be evicted. This helps maintain a balance between performance and memory usage.

4. Benefits of Caching:

- **Improved Performance:** Reduces data retrieval times by serving data directly from the cache.

- **Reduced Load on Backend Systems:** Caching reduces the number of requests hitting the database or other backend systems, which helps improve their overall performance and reduces operational costs.

- **Lower Latency:** Caching reduces round-trip times for data retrieval, resulting in faster response times for users.

Real-World Examples

1. Designing a Content Delivery Network (CDN):

Problem: Design a CDN that caches static content (images, videos, CSS, JavaScript) closer to end-users to reduce latency and improve website load times.

High-Level Design:

- **Distributed Caching:** Deploy multiple edge servers around the globe to store cached copies of static assets. These edge servers will be located closer to end-users to reduce the latency in fetching the data.

- **Load Balancing:** Use load balancers to route user requests to the nearest edge server. If an edge server is unavailable, the load balancer can route the traffic to a different server.

- **Content Replication:** Content (e.g., images, videos) is replicated and distributed across multiple locations. Popular content is cached at the edge servers, while less frequently accessed content can be pulled from the origin server.

- **Cache Invalidation:** Use cache expiration (TTL) or cache purging strategies to ensure content is updated when necessary. For example, if a user updates a profile image, the corresponding cache must be invalidated to serve the updated image.

- **CDN Providers:** Popular CDN providers include **Cloudflare, Akamai**, and **Amazon CloudFront**.

Scalability Considerations:

- The CDN can scale by adding more edge locations globally as the traffic volume grows. The system should handle large traffic spikes by utilizing additional caching layers at edge servers, reducing the load on the origin server.

2. Implementing Caching for a News Website:

Problem: A news website needs to cache article content, trending topics, and user-specific data (e.g., personalized recommendations) to improve performance and reduce the load on the database.

High-Level Design:

- **Cache Popular Content:** Cache the most viewed news articles, trending topics, and other static content like images and videos in an in-memory cache, using **Redis** or **Memcached**.

- **Cache User-Specific Data:** For personalized recommendations, cache user-specific data (e.g., recommended articles) and update it periodically using background jobs.

- **Cache-Aside Strategy:** When a user requests an article, the system first checks if the article is available in the cache. If it's not, it fetches the article from the database, caches it, and then serves it to the user.

- **Write-Through Cache:** When new articles are published, the system writes the article to both the database and the cache to keep data in sync.

- **Cache Expiration:** Set a TTL (Time To Live) for cached data such as articles, so outdated content is refreshed periodically, ensuring that users always see up-to-date news.

Scalability Considerations:

- As the number of articles and users grows, the caching layer must scale horizontally. The cache should be distributed across multiple servers to handle the increasing load, with **Redis Cluster** or similar distributed caching solutions.

- Implementing **load balancing** for the web servers ensures that requests for cached content are distributed evenly, preventing bottlenecks and ensuring high availability.

Conclusion

Load balancing and **caching** are two critical techniques for optimizing the performance, scalability, and reliability of distributed systems. **Load balancing** helps distribute traffic evenly across multiple servers, ensuring high availability and improved resource utilization. **Caching** accelerates data retrieval and reduces the load on backend systems, significantly improving response times and reducing latency. In this chapter, we've discussed the core principles of load balancing and caching and provided real-world examples like **designing a CDN** and **implementing caching for a news website**. By mastering these techniques, you can build high-performance, scalable systems capable of handling large volumes of traffic while maintaining a seamless user experience.

CHAPTER 20

SECURITY AND AUTHENTICATION IN SYSTEM DESIGN

Security is one of the most critical concerns in system design, especially when handling sensitive user data and integrating with third-party services. A well-designed system must ensure that it is resilient to attacks, protects sensitive data, and maintains the integrity and availability of services. In this chapter, we will explore common **security considerations** in system design, approaches for securing **APIs**, **databases**, and **user data**, and real-world examples like **implementing OAuth for authentication** and **securing payment systems**.

Common Security Considerations in System Design

When designing a system, it's essential to consider security at every level of the architecture. Some of the most common security considerations include:

223

1. Data Privacy and Encryption:

- Protecting sensitive data, such as user personal information and payment details, is crucial for maintaining privacy and meeting regulatory requirements (e.g., GDPR, CCPA).
- Use **encryption** to protect data both at rest and in transit:
  - **At Rest:** Encrypt sensitive data stored in databases, file systems, or cloud storage using algorithms like **AES-256**.
  - **In Transit:** Use **TLS/SSL** (Transport Layer Security) to encrypt data transmitted over the network, ensuring that sensitive information (e.g., passwords, credit card numbers) cannot be intercepted.

2. Authentication and Authorization:

- **Authentication** ensures that users are who they claim to be (e.g., logging in with a username and password).
- **Authorization** defines what authenticated users are allowed to do (e.g., viewing certain pages, modifying data).

- Use strong authentication mechanisms (e.g., **OAuth, JWT, Multi-factor Authentication**) to ensure only authorized users can access the system.

3. Input Validation and Sanitization:

- To prevent attacks like **SQL injection, cross-site scripting (XSS)**, and **cross-site request forgery (CSRF)**, it's essential to validate and sanitize all user inputs.
- Use techniques such as **parameterized queries** and **input sanitization libraries** to protect against malicious input.

4. Access Control:

- Implement **role-based access control (RBAC)** or **attribute-based access control (ABAC)** to ensure users can only access resources they're authorized to view or modify.
- Apply the **principle of least privilege**, ensuring that users and systems have only the permissions they need to perform their tasks.

5. Session Management:

- **Session management** is essential for maintaining a secure user experience, especially in web applications.
- Use **secure cookies** with the HttpOnly and Secure flags to prevent **session hijacking** and ensure that sessions are invalidated after a set period of inactivity.

6. Logging and Monitoring:

- Continuously monitor system activity for suspicious behavior, unauthorized access attempts, or abnormal patterns that may indicate a security breach.
- Implement **audit logs** for sensitive actions (e.g., login attempts, data modifications) to help track and respond to potential security incidents.

Approaches for Securing APIs, Databases, and User Data

1. Securing APIs:

APIs are often the primary method of communication between different parts of a system or with external services, making them a critical security component.

- **Use HTTPS for All API Traffic:** Secure your APIs with **SSL/TLS** to ensure that data exchanged between the client and server is encrypted.
- **API Authentication:**
  - Use **OAuth 2.0** or **JWT (JSON Web Tokens)** to authenticate and authorize API requests. OAuth 2.0 is widely used for secure authorization, allowing third-party apps to access user data without exposing credentials.
  - For internal APIs, consider using **API keys** or **Mutual TLS** for client authentication.
- **Rate Limiting and Throttling:**
  - Protect your APIs from abuse and DDoS attacks by implementing **rate limiting** and **throttling**. For example, allow only a certain number of requests per minute or hour to prevent overloading the system.
- **Access Control for APIs:**
  - Implement **role-based access control (RBAC)** in your API to ensure that users can only access the resources or perform actions that they are authorized to do.

o Use API gateways like **Kong** or **AWS API Gateway** to enforce security policies and authentication for your APIs.

2. Securing Databases:

Databases are often the most valuable target for attackers since they store sensitive user and system data. Ensuring database security is critical to the integrity and privacy of the system.

- **Encryption:**
  - o Use **encryption at rest** to protect stored data from unauthorized access.
  - o **Field-level encryption** can be used for particularly sensitive fields, such as passwords and credit card numbers.
- **Database Authentication:**
  - o Ensure that the database uses **strong authentication mechanisms**, such as username/password, public key infrastructure (PKI), or integration with an identity provider.
- **Access Control:**

- o Use **database roles** and **permissions** to restrict who can view, modify, or delete data.
- o Implement **least privilege** access control to ensure that users can only access the specific data they need.

- **Audit Logging:**
  - o Enable **audit logging** to track access to the database, including who accessed what data and when. This can help in identifying and mitigating potential security breaches.

3. Securing User Data:

User data is one of the most sensitive pieces of information your system will handle, so it's essential to protect it rigorously.

- **Password Management:**
  - o Always **hash passwords** using a strong hashing algorithm such as **bcrypt, PBKDF2,** or **Argon2**. Never store passwords in plaintext.
  - o Use **salted hashes** to protect against **rainbow table attacks**.
- **Multi-Factor Authentication (MFA):**

- Enforce **MFA** for all users, especially for accessing sensitive parts of the system. This adds an additional layer of security by requiring something the user knows (password) and something they have (mobile device, authenticator app).

- **User Data Encryption:**
  - Encrypt sensitive user data such as **Social Security numbers, credit card details**, and **health information** both in transit and at rest.

Real-World Examples

1. Implementing OAuth for Authentication:

Problem: You need to allow users to log into your application using their Google or Facebook accounts, without storing their passwords.

OAuth Implementation:

- **Authorization Code Flow (for web apps):**
  1. **User initiates login:** The user clicks the "Login with Google" button.

2. **Redirect to OAuth provider:** The app redirects the user to Google's OAuth authorization server.

3. **User grants permission:** The user logs in to Google and grants permission to access their profile.

4. **Authorization code:** Google redirects the user back to your app with an authorization code.

5. **Exchange authorization code for tokens:** Your app exchanges the authorization code for an **access token** and **refresh token**.

6. **API access:** Use the access token to call the Google API on behalf of the user and retrieve their profile data.

OAuth provides secure, token-based authentication and is widely used in modern web applications, ensuring that user credentials are not stored or exposed by the application.

2. Securing Payment Systems:

Problem: You need to secure a payment system that allows users to make purchases using their credit card.

High-Level Design:

- **Payment Gateway Integration:**
  - Integrate a secure third-party **payment gateway** like **Stripe, PayPal,** or **Square** for handling payments. These services ensure that sensitive payment data (credit card numbers) are never stored on your servers.
  - Use **tokenization** to replace sensitive payment information with a unique token that can be safely stored and used for future transactions.

- **PCI DSS Compliance:**
  - Ensure your payment system complies with the **Payment Card Industry Data Security Standard (PCI DSS).** This includes encryption of sensitive data, implementing strong authentication, and conducting regular security audits.

- **SSL/TLS Encryption:**
  - Use **SSL/TLS** to encrypt data sent between the user's browser and your server, preventing sensitive payment data from being intercepted during transmission.

- **Multi-Factor Authentication:**

o Use **MFA** for users accessing sensitive payment information to ensure that only authorized users can make transactions.

Conclusion

Security and authentication are essential considerations in the design of any system. From **encrypting sensitive data** to **implementing strong authentication mechanisms** like **OAuth**, securing your APIs, databases, and user data ensures that your system is resilient to attacks and protects user privacy. In this chapter, we discussed common security considerations, approaches for securing various components of a system, and real-world examples like **OAuth for authentication** and **securing payment systems**. By incorporating these security best practices into your system design, you can create safe, reliable, and compliant systems that protect both your users and your organization.

CHAPTER 21

MONITORING AND SCALING SYSTEMS

As applications grow and evolve, ensuring that they perform well under increasing loads and that any potential issues are detected early becomes paramount. **Monitoring** systems and implementing strategies for **scaling** them effectively are key practices for ensuring the long-term success and reliability of an application. In this chapter, we'll explore how to monitor systems for performance and errors, strategies for scaling systems to handle growing traffic, and real-world examples such as **auto-scaling instances in the cloud** and using monitoring tools like **Prometheus** and **Grafana**.

How to Monitor Systems for Performance and Errors

1. What is Monitoring?

- **Monitoring** is the process of continuously observing and recording the performance, availability, and overall health of a system. It involves tracking system metrics, logs, and alerts to identify and address issues proactively.

- Effective monitoring helps to:
  o Detect **performance bottlenecks** or spikes in resource usage.
  o Identify **errors or failures** in real time, allowing for quick response and resolution.
  o Ensure **high availability** and optimal performance by tracking key metrics and thresholds.

2. Key Metrics to Monitor:

- **System Metrics:**
  o **CPU Utilization:** Tracks the percentage of CPU resources used by the system. High CPU usage may indicate inefficient processes or resource bottlenecks.
  o **Memory Usage:** Monitors the amount of memory being consumed by the application. Memory leaks or insufficient memory allocation can lead to performance degradation or crashes.
  o **Disk I/O:** Measures the rate at which data is read from and written to storage. High disk

235

I/O can be a sign of inefficient database queries or excessive logging.

- o **Network Traffic:** Tracks incoming and outgoing traffic, including bandwidth and latency. High network traffic can indicate either healthy system usage or a potential DDoS attack.

- **Application Metrics:**
  - o **Request Latency:** Measures the time taken to process a request from the client to the server. Monitoring request latency helps identify slow or bottlenecked parts of the application.
  - o **Error Rate:** Tracks the number of errors (e.g., HTTP 500 responses or database connection failures) in the system. A high error rate often indicates problems with the application or infrastructure.
  - o **Throughput:** Measures the number of requests or transactions the system processes per unit of time. Monitoring throughput can help assess the load and efficiency of the system.

- **Service-Specific Metrics:**

- o **Database Queries:** Tracks the number of database queries, query execution time, and database response time.

- o **Cache Hit/Miss Rate:** Measures how often data is found in the cache compared to being fetched from the underlying database. A low cache hit rate may indicate inefficient caching.

3. Monitoring Tools:

- **Prometheus:** A powerful open-source monitoring and alerting toolkit. It collects and stores time-series data, such as CPU usage, memory utilization, and application-specific metrics. Prometheus allows users to query data and set up alerting rules to notify teams when specific thresholds are exceeded.

- **Grafana:** A visualization tool that integrates with Prometheus and other data sources to create dashboards for visualizing system performance metrics. Grafana allows teams to monitor real-time system health and performance trends.

- **ELK Stack (Elasticsearch, Logstash, Kibana):** Used for aggregating and analyzing logs. Logs can

237

be collected using Logstash, stored in Elasticsearch, and visualized with Kibana.

- **Datadog, New Relic, and Splunk:** Cloud-based monitoring solutions that offer more advanced features, such as application performance monitoring (APM), log aggregation, and anomaly detection.

4. Alerts and Thresholds:

- Set up **alerts** to notify the relevant teams when key performance indicators (KPIs) reach critical thresholds. For example:
  - High CPU usage (e.g., > 90%) might trigger an alert.
  - Error rate spikes (e.g., > 5% 500 status codes) could trigger an error alert.
- Alerts can be configured to be sent via email, SMS, or integrated communication tools like **Slack**.

Strategies for Scaling Systems to Handle Growing Traffic

As traffic to your system increases, you need to ensure that it can scale to handle the load without performance degradation. **Scalability** involves adapting the system architecture to support growing traffic by adding resources and optimizing the existing infrastructure.

1. Horizontal Scaling (Scaling Out):

- **Definition:** Horizontal scaling involves adding more servers or instances to the system to distribute the load across multiple machines.
- **How It Works:**
  - For web applications, add more web server instances behind a **load balancer** to distribute incoming traffic evenly.
  - For databases, use **sharding** (partitioning data across multiple databases) and **replication** (duplicating data across multiple servers) to ensure that the database can handle more read and write operations.
- **Benefits:**
  - More cost-effective than vertical scaling for large-scale applications.
  - Offers high availability and fault tolerance, as traffic is distributed across multiple nodes.

2. Vertical Scaling (Scaling Up):

- **Definition:** Vertical scaling involves upgrading the hardware of existing servers by adding more CPU, memory, or storage.
- **How It Works:**
  - Increase the capacity of your database, application server, or web server by adding more resources to individual machines.
- **Limitations:**
  - Vertical scaling can only go so far before you hit the physical limits of the hardware.
  - It may be more expensive than horizontal scaling for handling large amounts of traffic.

3. Auto-Scaling:

- **Definition:** Auto-scaling dynamically adjusts the number of running instances based on traffic demand. It is commonly used in cloud environments (e.g., AWS EC2 Auto Scaling, Azure VM Scale Sets).
- **How It Works:**
  - The system automatically adds or removes instances based on predefined scaling policies. For example, if traffic increases beyond a certain threshold, new instances are

spun up; if traffic decreases, instances are terminated.

- **Benefits:**
  - o Ensures optimal resource utilization, scaling up during high traffic and scaling down during low traffic, thereby saving costs.

4. Database Scaling:

- **Horizontal Scaling (Sharding):** Partition your database across multiple servers to handle a growing amount of data and read/write requests.
- **Read Replicas:** Use read replicas to offload read-heavy operations from the master database. This ensures that the database can handle a higher volume of traffic without becoming a bottleneck.
- **Database Caching:** Implement **in-memory caches** (e.g., Redis or Memcached) to reduce the load on databases by storing frequently accessed data in memory.

5. Content Delivery Networks (CDNs):

- Use a CDN to distribute static content (e.g., images, videos, JavaScript files) across multiple edge locations globally. This ensures faster content delivery to users, reducing load on your origin server and improving performance.

Real-World Examples

1. Auto-Scaling Instances in the Cloud:

Problem: A website is experiencing spikes in traffic during certain events (e.g., sales, product launches) and needs to handle these spikes without manual intervention.

Solution:

- **Auto-Scaling in AWS:**
  - Set up an **Auto Scaling Group** in AWS to automatically adjust the number of EC2 instances based on traffic demand.
  - Define scaling policies based on **CPU utilization** (e.g., if CPU usage exceeds 80%, add more instances) or **network traffic** (e.g., if network traffic is above a certain threshold, scale out).

- o Use an **Elastic Load Balancer** (ELB) to distribute traffic evenly across the EC2 instances.
- o The system automatically scales up during peak times (e.g., sales events) and scales down during low-traffic periods, ensuring cost efficiency and high availability.

2. Using Monitoring Tools like Prometheus and Grafana:

Problem: A cloud-based microservices application needs to monitor various metrics (e.g., CPU usage, memory usage, application errors, and service latency) across a distributed architecture.

Solution:

- **Prometheus:**
  - o Set up **Prometheus** to collect time-series metrics from your microservices by scraping them at regular intervals.
  - o Configure Prometheus to collect application-level metrics, such as request rates, error rates, and latencies.

- o Store the metrics in Prometheus' time-series database for querying and alerting.
- **Grafana:**
  - o Use **Grafana** to create interactive dashboards for visualizing metrics collected by Prometheus. Display system health, service performance, and error rates in real-time.
  - o Set up **alerts in Grafana** to notify the operations team when metrics exceed predefined thresholds (e.g., when error rates go above a certain percentage or latency exceeds a threshold).

Outcome:

- The team can monitor the system's performance, set up alerts for potential issues, and ensure the system runs smoothly during periods of high traffic or when an issue arises.

Conclusion

Effective **monitoring** and **scaling** strategies are essential for building robust systems that can handle increasing traffic while maintaining performance and reliability. By monitoring key metrics and using tools like **Prometheus** and **Grafana**, you can gain insights into your system's performance and address issues proactively. **Scaling strategies**, such as **horizontal scaling, auto-scaling**, and **CDNs**, ensure that your system can handle growing demands and provide a smooth experience for users. By mastering these practices, you can ensure that your system remains efficient, responsive, and available under any conditions.

CHAPTER 22

BEHAVIORAL QUESTIONS - PREPARING FOR THE SOFT SKILLS INTERVIEW

In addition to technical skills, **soft skills** play a crucial role in determining whether a candidate is a good fit for a team or organization. **Behavioral questions** are commonly asked in **tech interviews** to assess these interpersonal skills, work ethic, and decision-making processes. In this chapter, we will explore the importance of behavioral questions in tech interviews, common types of behavioral questions such as those related to **leadership**, **problem-solving**, and **conflict resolution**, and real-world examples of how to answer them effectively.

Understanding the Importance of Behavioral Questions in Tech Interviews

1. Assessing Cultural Fit:

- Behavioral questions allow interviewers to understand how a candidate might fit within the company culture. These questions provide insights into how candidates approach teamwork, handle challenges, and align with the organization's values and mission.

- **Example:** A company that values collaboration may ask about a time when you worked with a team to overcome a challenge, evaluating your ability to collaborate and communicate effectively.

2. Evaluating Problem-Solving and Critical Thinking:

- While technical questions test your expertise in coding and system design, behavioral questions reveal how you approach real-world problems, make decisions under pressure, and navigate complex situations.

- **Example:** An interviewer might ask about a situation where you faced a difficult technical problem and how you resolved it, testing your critical thinking and resourcefulness.

3. Demonstrating Soft Skills:

- Tech companies value strong **communication**, **leadership**, and **empathy** skills, which can be crucial in managing teams, handling clients, or mentoring junior staff. Behavioral questions are an effective way to assess these traits.

- **Example:** A common question about conflict resolution will help the interviewer gauge your ability to maintain a positive working environment, even when disagreements arise.

Common Types of Behavioral Questions

Behavioral questions can cover a variety of topics. Here are the most common categories and types of behavioral questions you may encounter in a tech interview:

1. Leadership Questions:

- Leadership questions assess your ability to take initiative, motivate others, and manage teams or projects. Even if you aren't applying for a managerial position, interviewers may ask leadership-related questions to see how you take responsibility and inspire your team.

- **Common Questions:**
  - "Tell me about a time when you led a team through a challenging project."
  - "Describe a situation where you had to motivate a team that was struggling to meet deadlines."
  - "Can you give an example of a time when you took the initiative to improve a process at work?"

2. Problem-Solving Questions:

- These questions explore your ability to tackle complex challenges, think critically, and find effective solutions. Problem-solving questions can be related to technical or non-technical situations.
- **Common Questions:**
  - "Tell me about a time when you encountered a significant technical problem and how you resolved it."
  - "Describe a situation in which you had to find a creative solution to a problem at work."
  - "Give an example of when you had to learn something new quickly to solve a problem."

3. Conflict Resolution Questions:

- Conflict resolution questions test your ability to handle disagreements, manage conflicts within a team, and maintain a positive working environment.
- **Common Questions:**
  - "Tell me about a time when you disagreed with a team member and how you handled it."
  - "Describe a situation where you had to mediate a conflict between two colleagues."
  - "Have you ever faced a difficult situation with a supervisor or client? How did you resolve it?"

4. Teamwork and Collaboration Questions:

- These questions assess how well you work with others, especially in diverse teams, and how you contribute to the overall success of a project.
- **Common Questions:**
  - "Describe a time when you had to collaborate with a cross-functional team."
  - "Tell me about a project you worked on that required close teamwork. How did you contribute?"

o "Can you share an example of how you handled working with someone with a very different working style?"

5. Time Management and Prioritization Questions:

- Time management questions test your ability to balance multiple tasks, prioritize effectively, and meet deadlines.
- **Common Questions:**
  - o "Tell me about a time when you had to manage multiple deadlines. How did you prioritize your tasks?"
  - o "Describe a situation where you had too many tasks to handle. How did you decide what to focus on first?"
  - o "Can you provide an example of when you successfully managed a project with competing priorities?"

Real-World Examples of How to Answer Behavioral Questions Effectively

When answering behavioral questions, the **STAR method** (Situation, Task, Action, Result) is a useful framework to structure your responses. This method helps you provide clear, concise, and complete answers that demonstrate your skills and experience.

1. STAR Method Breakdown:

- **Situation:** Describe the context and background of the situation.
- **Task:** Explain the task or challenge you were facing.
- **Action:** Describe the specific actions you took to address the situation.
- **Result:** Share the outcome of your actions, including any measurable achievements.

Let's go through real-world examples of how to apply the STAR method in answering behavioral questions.

Example 1: Leadership Question

- **Question:** "Tell me about a time when you led a team through a challenging project."

Answer using STAR:

o **Situation:** "I was leading a team of four engineers on a project to develop a new feature for our SaaS product. The project had tight deadlines and required significant coordination with the product and design teams."

o **Task:** "The main challenge was to ensure that the feature was delivered on time while maintaining high-quality standards. Our team had to work closely with others who had different priorities."

o **Action:** "I held weekly meetings to track progress, identify roadblocks, and keep everyone aligned. I also stepped in to resolve any conflicts between team members and acted as the main point of contact with stakeholders to manage expectations."

o **Result:** "We successfully launched the feature on time and received positive feedback from the product team. The feature led to a 15% increase in user engagement over the next quarter."

Example 2: Problem-Solving Question

- **Question:** "Tell me about a time when you encountered a significant technical problem and how you resolved it."

  Answer using STAR:

  o **Situation:** "During the launch of a new web application, we noticed that page load times were unusually high, especially during peak usage times."

  o **Task:** "I was responsible for diagnosing the root cause of the issue and implementing a solution to improve performance."

  o **Action:** "I analyzed the server logs and identified that the database queries were not optimized, causing delays. I implemented query optimizations and introduced database indexing to speed up data retrieval. Additionally, I implemented caching to reduce the load on the database."

  o **Result:** "The performance improved significantly, and page load times decreased by 50%. The users experienced a smoother experience, and we saw a 20% reduction in bounce rates during high-traffic periods."

Example 3: Conflict Resolution Question

- **Question:** "Tell me about a time when you disagreed with a team member and how you handled it."

   Answer using STAR:

   o **Situation:** "In one project, a team member and I disagreed on the design approach for a feature. They wanted to implement a more complex solution, while I believed a simpler, more cost-effective approach would suffice."

   o **Task:** "We needed to come to a resolution quickly so that the project could continue on schedule without any delays."

   o **Action:** "I suggested we meet to discuss our points of view and find a middle ground. We reviewed the trade-offs of both approaches and analyzed the potential impact on the overall project timeline and budget. After the discussion, we agreed on a modified version of their solution, which kept things simple while adding some of their ideas for scalability."

○ **Result:** "The feature was delivered on time and within budget. The compromise worked well for the team, and we were able to implement additional optimizations in future projects."

Conclusion

Behavioral questions are an essential part of tech interviews because they help interviewers assess how candidates handle various real-world situations, such as leadership, problem-solving, conflict resolution, and teamwork. By preparing for these questions using the **STAR method**, you can provide clear, structured answers that demonstrate your skills, experience, and ability to navigate challenging situations. Whether you're discussing a technical challenge, a leadership experience, or resolving a conflict, understanding how to frame your responses in a compelling way will help you stand out as a well-rounded candidate who can succeed in a collaborative work environment.

CHAPTER 23

PROBLEM-SOLVING APPROACH - SOLVING CODING PROBLEMS IN INTERVIEWS

In coding interviews, candidates are often presented with problems that test their ability to think critically and solve challenges under time pressure. A structured problem-solving approach is essential for tackling these problems effectively. In this chapter, we will outline a step-by-step approach to solving coding problems in interviews, cover how to break down problems, write code, and test solutions, and provide real-world examples from popular coding platforms like **Leetcode**, **HackerRank**, and **CodeSignal**.

A Step-by-Step Approach to Solving Coding Problems

1. Understand the Problem:

- **Read the Problem Statement Carefully:** Before jumping into the solution, ensure you completely understand the problem. Pay attention to key details such as input and output formats, constraints, and edge cases.

- **Clarify Ambiguities:** If something in the problem is unclear or vague, ask the interviewer questions to get more context. This helps you avoid making incorrect assumptions and wasting time.
  - o Example questions:
    - "What is the range of values for the input?"
    - "Are there any specific constraints on time or memory?"

2. Plan the Solution:

- **Identify the Problem Type:** Is it an array problem? A string manipulation problem? A graph traversal? Understanding the type of problem helps you know which algorithms or data structures might be applicable.
- **Think of a Brute-Force Solution:** Often, starting with a brute-force approach can help you understand the problem and give you a baseline solution.
  - o Example: If the problem asks you to find the maximum value in an unsorted array, the

brute-force solution would be to iterate through all elements and compare them.

- **Optimize the Approach:** Once you have a brute-force solution, think about ways to optimize it. Look for patterns, ways to reduce redundant work, or better algorithms.

  o Example: In the array problem, you might realize that using a divide-and-conquer approach (like sorting) or leveraging a data structure (like a heap) could improve the efficiency.

3. Write the Code:

- **Start with a Skeleton:** Before diving into coding, outline the structure of your solution. Define the function signature, and consider how you will handle inputs and outputs.

- **Write Incrementally:** Start by coding small parts of the solution. Don't try to write the entire solution in one go. Write small functions or steps, test them, and then build on them.

- **Use Comments and Pseudocode:** If you're unsure of how to implement a part of the solution, write down your approach in pseudocode first. Use comments in your code to explain each step of the logic.

4. Test the Code:

- **Use Example Inputs:** Test your solution against example inputs provided in the problem statement. This is an essential first step to ensure your solution works for the basic cases.
- **Edge Cases:** Identify and test edge cases. These might include:
    - Empty inputs (e.g., an empty array or string).
    - Large inputs (e.g., large arrays, large numbers).
    - Special values (e.g., 0, -1, null, NaN).
- **Iterate and Debug:** If the solution doesn't pass a test case, don't panic. Go back to your code and debug step-by-step. Use **print statements** or a **debugger** to check where things go wrong.

5. Communicate Your Thought Process:

- Throughout the interview, clearly explain your approach to the interviewer. Walk them through how you plan to solve the problem, why you're choosing a particular algorithm or data structure, and how you'll handle edge cases.

- **Explain trade-offs:** If you're making assumptions or trade-offs (e.g., choosing space efficiency over time efficiency), explain these decisions to the interviewer.

How to Break Down Problems, Write Code, and Test Solutions in an Interview

1. Breaking Down the Problem:

- **Identify Inputs and Outputs:** Focus on the data you're given and the result you need to compute. Understand the constraints and the range of valid inputs. This will guide your choice of algorithm and data structures.

- **Identify Key Operations:** Break the problem down into smaller operations. For example, if you're sorting an array, the key operation is comparing and swapping elements.

- **Handle Edge Cases:** Consider scenarios where the input might be empty, too large, or contain special values. Identifying these edge cases early on can save you time later.

2. Writing Code:

- **Start Small:** Begin by coding small pieces and test them often. Don't try to write everything at once. Build, test, and debug incrementally.
- **Maintain Readable Code:** Write code that is easy to understand. Use descriptive variable names, and structure your code logically.
- **Avoid Over-Optimizing Initially:** Focus on getting a working solution first. Once that's in place, you can revisit it to improve performance or simplify the logic.

3. Testing and Refining the Solution:

- **Test with Provided Inputs:** Run the solution against the test cases provided in the problem description to confirm that it works.
- **Test with Edge Cases:** Manually think of and test edge cases that may break your solution, such as:
  - Empty or null inputs.
  - Very large or very small numbers.

- Unusual character sequences for string-based problems.

- **Optimize If Needed:** Once your code passes all test cases, evaluate its time and space complexity. If it is inefficient, consider ways to optimize it. Use **Big O notation** to communicate the efficiency of your solution.

Real-World Examples: Solving Problems from Popular Coding Platforms

Let's look at some examples of problems you might encounter on coding platforms like **LeetCode**, **HackerRank**, and **CodeSignal**, and walk through the process of solving them.

1. LeetCode Example: Two Sum

Problem: Given an array of integers and a target number, return the indices of the two numbers that add up to the target.

Step-by-Step Approach:

- **Understand the problem:** We need to find two numbers in the array whose sum equals the target and return their indices.

- **Brute-Force Solution:** A naive solution would be to use two nested loops to check all pairs of numbers in the array. This gives us a time complexity of $O(n2)O(n^2)O(n2)$.

- **Optimized Solution:** We can use a **hash map** to store the difference between the target and each number as we iterate through the array. This allows us to check if the complementary number (target - current number) exists in the map, reducing the time complexity to $O(n)O(n)O(n)$.

Code:

python

```python
def twoSum(nums, target):
    num_map = {}
    for i, num in enumerate(nums):
        complement = target - num
        if complement in num_map:
            return [num_map[complement], i]
        num_map[num] = i
```

Testing:

- Test with the input: nums = [2, 7, 11, 15], target = 9.
  The output should be [0, 1] because nums[0] +
  nums[1] = 9.

---

2. HackerRank Example: Counting Valleys

Problem: A hiker is walking in the mountains, and you need
to determine how many valleys they walk through based on
their elevation change.

Step-by-Step Approach:

- **Understand the problem:** We need to track the
  hiker's elevation and count how many times they go
  below sea level and then return to sea level.
- **Plan:** Start from sea level and track the elevation.
  Count a valley every time the hiker descends below
  sea level and then comes back to sea level.

Code:

python

```
def countingValleys(n, s):
    elevation = 0
    valleys = 0
    for step in s:
        if step == 'D':
            elevation -= 1
        if step == 'U':
            elevation += 1
            if elevation == 0:
                valleys += 1
    return valleys
```

Testing:

- Test with the input: n = 8, s = "UDDDUDUU". The output should be 1, as there is one valley.

---

3. CodeSignal Example: Add Two Digits

Problem: Given a two-digit number, find the sum of its digits.

Step-by-Step Approach:

- **Understand the problem:** We need to extract the digits from the number and compute their sum.
- **Plan:** Extract the tens and ones digits, then sum them up.

Code:

python

```
def addTwoDigits(n):
    return sum(map(int, str(n)))
```

Testing:

- Test with the input: n = 29. The output should be 11, as 2 + 9 = 11.

Conclusion

Solving coding problems in interviews requires a systematic approach that includes understanding the problem, planning a solution, writing clean code, and thoroughly testing it. The **STAR method** (Situation, Task, Action, Result) can also be applied when explaining your thought process and demonstrating how you arrived at a solution. By practicing coding problems from platforms like **LeetCode**, **HackerRank**, and **CodeSignal**, you can refine your problem-solving skills and improve your chances of succeeding in technical interviews.

CHAPTER 24

MOCK INTERVIEWS AND PRACTICE - BUILDING CONFIDENCE

One of the most important aspects of preparing for technical interviews is **practice**. While studying algorithms, data structures, and problem-solving techniques is essential, it's equally important to simulate real interview conditions through **mock interviews**. Mock interviews help you get accustomed to the interview format, build confidence, and improve your ability to perform under pressure. In this chapter, we'll explore the importance of mock interviews, how to simulate real interview conditions, and tips for staying calm and performing well under pressure.

The Importance of Mock Interviews and Consistent Practice

1. Mimicking Real-World Conditions:

- **Mock interviews** simulate the actual environment of a real interview, helping you become comfortable with the pressure and time constraints. They allow you to practice verbalizing your thought process, solving problems on the spot, and handling feedback from an interviewer.

- Practicing in realistic conditions allows you to anticipate common challenges in interviews, such as dealing with complex questions, navigating gaps in knowledge, or working under a time crunch.

2. Identifying Weaknesses:

- While doing coding problems by yourself can help you learn concepts and algorithms, mock interviews help identify weaknesses in your performance. You may realize that you have trouble explaining your thought process, struggle to write code in front of someone, or get stuck on specific types of questions.
- By recognizing these areas early, you can work on improving them before your actual interview.

3. Building Confidence:

- Mock interviews allow you to practice presenting your solutions confidently. The more you practice, the more comfortable you will become with discussing your approach, answering follow-up questions, and handling feedback.

- Building confidence is crucial because confidence plays a key role in managing nervousness and staying focused during a real interview.

4. Feedback and Improvement:

- Feedback from mock interviewers is invaluable. Constructive feedback helps you understand what you did well and what areas need improvement. This feedback is critical in refining your interviewing skills, adjusting your approach, and gaining insights into your performance.

How to Simulate Real Interview Conditions and Get Feedback

1. Setting Up Mock Interviews:

- **Schedule Mock Interviews with Peers or Mentors:**
  o One of the best ways to simulate real interview conditions is to conduct mock interviews with a peer or mentor who has

experience with technical interviews. This provides you with real-time feedback, mimicking the dynamics of a real interview.

o Platforms like **Pramp, Interviewing.io**, and **Gainlo** allow you to connect with interviewers or peers to practice in a structured, realistic setting.

- **Use Online Interview Platforms:**

  o Many coding platforms (e.g., **LeetCode, HackerRank, CodeSignal**) offer **interview simulation** features that simulate time constraints and provide automatic feedback on coding problems. These tools can help you practice solving problems within a set time frame, just like a real interview.

  o **Mock interview platforms** such as **Exercism, Coderbyte**, and **Codewars** also offer opportunities to practice coding problems while getting feedback on your solutions.

2. Simulate Real Interview Conditions:

- **Time Constraints:** Set a strict time limit (usually 30-45 minutes) for each problem to simulate the pressure of a timed interview. Avoid spending too much time on any one problem.

- **Verbalizing Your Thought Process:** During mock interviews, practice **speaking your thoughts aloud** as you solve problems. This helps improve your ability to explain your approach and makes you more comfortable with verbal communication during the actual interview.

- **Simulate a Remote Interview:** If your real interview is likely to be remote (e.g., via Zoom or Google Meet), practice mock interviews using video conferencing tools. This helps you adjust to the challenges of remote communication, such as technical glitches or speaking through a screen.

- **Behavioral Questions:** In addition to coding problems, mock interviews should also include **behavioral questions** to help you prepare for assessing soft skills. Practice answering questions about teamwork, problem-solving, and conflict resolution to demonstrate your interpersonal skills.

3. Getting Feedback:

- **Self-Reflection:** After each mock interview, take some time to reflect on your performance. Identify areas where you struggled, whether it was in communicating your thought process, coding efficiently, or staying calm under pressure.

- **Feedback from Interviewers:** Ask your mock interviewers for specific feedback on areas where you can improve. For example:
  - o Did I explain my approach clearly?
  - o Was my code efficient and readable?
  - o Did I manage my time effectively?
  - o Was I able to handle tough questions well?
- **Peer Reviews:** When practicing with peers, ask them to give you honest, constructive feedback. Ensure that the feedback is actionable so you can work on improving specific aspects of your performance.

Tips for Staying Calm and Performing Well Under Pressure

1. Practice Mental Toughness:

- Interviews can be stressful, and it's normal to feel nervous, but learning to manage this stress is crucial for performing well.

- **Mindfulness Techniques:** Practice deep breathing or mindfulness exercises before mock interviews or actual interviews to calm your nerves.

- **Positive Visualization:** Before starting, visualize yourself succeeding in the interview. Positive visualization can help reduce anxiety and boost your confidence.

2. Break Down the Problem Step-by-Step:

- When faced with a coding problem, take a moment to think through it before diving into coding. Breaking the problem into smaller steps can help you stay focused and reduce the feeling of being overwhelmed.

- **Ask Clarifying Questions:** If you don't understand the problem or if it seems ambiguous, ask for clarification. Taking a few seconds to think through the problem can save you time and confusion later.

3. Manage Time Effectively:

- **Don't Get Stuck on One Problem:** If you get stuck, don't let it consume your time. Move on to the next step, and if necessary, explain to the interviewer that you're working through the issue. You can always come back to it later.

- **Practice Time Management:** During mock interviews, simulate time constraints to learn how to pace yourself. If you're struggling to solve a problem within the time limit, this is a sign you need to work on your efficiency.

4. Communicate Clearly and Effectively:

- **Think Aloud:** Always verbalize your thought process. Not only does it show the interviewer that you are actively thinking through the problem, but it also helps you stay organized.
- **Be Honest:** If you don't know the answer, it's better to admit it than to try and bluff your way through. Interviewers often appreciate honesty and the ability to stay calm in difficult situations.

5. Stay Positive and Don't Let Mistakes Derail You:

- It's easy to get discouraged after making a mistake, but **staying positive** and maintaining momentum is key. Mistakes are part of the process, and interviewers want to see how you handle setbacks.

- If you make an error, acknowledge it, correct it, and move forward. Demonstrating resilience is often more important than avoiding mistakes altogether.

Real-World Examples

1. Mock Interview Practice on LeetCode:

- **Problem:** "Given an array of integers, return the two numbers that add up to a target number."
- **Solution Process:**
  1. **Understand the Problem:** The input is an array of integers, and you need to return the indices of two numbers that sum up to a target.
  2. **Plan:** The brute-force solution would involve using two loops to check all pairs of numbers. The optimized solution uses a hash map to store previously seen numbers and check if the complement (target - number) is present.
  3. **Code the Solution:**

python

```
def twoSum(nums, target):
  num_map = {}
  for i, num in enumerate(nums):
    complement = target - num
    if complement in num_map:
      return [num_map[complement], i]
    num_map[num] = i
```

4. **Test the Solution:** Test on inputs like [2, 7, 11, 15] with a target of 9 to ensure the correct indices are returned.

2. Mock Interview Practice with a Peer on CodeSignal:

- **Problem:** "Write a function to check if a string is a palindrome."
- **Solution Process:**
  1. **Understand the Problem:** A palindrome is a word, phrase, or sequence that reads the same backward as forward. We need to check if a given string is one.
  2. **Plan:** Convert the string to lowercase and check if it reads the same forwards and backwards.
  3. **Code the Solution:**

python

```python
def isPalindrome(s):
    s = s.lower().replace(' ', '')
    return s == s[::-1]
```

4. **Test the Solution:** Test on inputs like "racecar" and "hello" to check if the solution works for both palindromes and non-palindromes.

Conclusion

Mock interviews and consistent **practice** are essential for building confidence and preparing for technical interviews. They help simulate real interview conditions, identify areas for improvement, and give you the opportunity to refine your problem-solving approach. By using mock interview platforms, receiving feedback, and following strategies for staying calm under pressure, you can greatly improve your performance in real interviews. Ultimately, success in interviews is not just about technical proficiency but also about how you manage time, communicate your thought process, and stay resilient in challenging situations.

CHAPTER 25

INTERVIEW ETIQUETTE AND COMMUNICATION SKILLS

In technical interviews, the ability to **communicate clearly** and present yourself professionally is just as important as solving the problem correctly. **Interview etiquette** and effective **communication skills** can significantly impact your success. How you approach the problem, explain your thought process, and interact with the interviewer will shape their perception of your problem-solving abilities, teamwork, and professionalism. In this chapter, we will discuss how to communicate your thought process during coding interviews, the importance of clarity and transparency, and non-verbal communication and professional presentation.

How to Communicate Your Thought Process During Coding Interviews

1. Verbalizing Your Thought Process:

- **Why It's Important:** One of the most crucial aspects of coding interviews is the ability to clearly articulate your thought process. Interviewers are not only interested in whether you can solve the problem but also how you approach and reason through it. Verbalizing your thought process allows interviewers to see your problem-solving skills, logical thinking, and ability to break down complex tasks.

- **How to Do It:**
  - **Start with a High-Level Overview:** Before diving into the code, explain what the problem is asking and your approach to solving it. This shows the interviewer that you understand the problem.
    - Example: "We need to find two numbers in this array that add up to a target sum. My approach will be to iterate through the array and check if the complement of the current number exists in a hash map."
  - **Describe Each Step:** As you write the code, explain each decision you make. For example, why you chose a specific data

structure, what each function does, and how you're handling edge cases.

- Example: "I'm using a hash map here because it allows us to look up values in constant time, which will make the solution more efficient than a nested loop approach."

o **Think Aloud:** If you encounter a challenge or need to make a decision, verbalize your reasoning. This demonstrates that you are actively thinking about the problem and are open to feedback or suggestions.

- Example: "I'm not sure if this approach will be optimal because we might be using too much memory. I'll try implementing it this way and then revisit it if needed."

2. Asking Clarifying Questions:

- If the problem is ambiguous or there are aspects you don't understand, ask **clarifying questions**. This not only shows that you are thorough but also helps you avoid making assumptions that could lead to mistakes.

- Example: "Are there any constraints on the size of the input array?" or "Should we handle negative numbers or zero in a special way?"
- Asking for clarification also demonstrates your **attention to detail** and ensures that you're solving the right problem.

3. Explaining Trade-offs and Decisions:

- If you are choosing between multiple approaches, explain the **trade-offs** involved. This shows the interviewer that you understand the pros and cons of different solutions.
  - Example: "I could use a brute-force approach with nested loops, but that would result in a time complexity of $O(n^2)$. Instead, I'm going with a hash map, which gives us a time complexity of $O(n)$ at the expense of using more memory."

The Importance of Clarity and Transparency When Solving Problems

1. Clear and Structured Solutions:

- **Organize Your Thoughts:** Interviewers appreciate a clear, structured approach to solving problems. Break the problem into smaller parts, solve them one at a time, and explain each step clearly.

- **Avoid Overcomplicating the Solution:** While it's tempting to use advanced algorithms or data structures, sometimes the simplest solution is the best. Avoid overengineering the solution, especially if it's not necessary for solving the problem effectively.

2. Transparency and Honesty:

- **Don't Be Afraid to Admit Mistakes:** If you make a mistake or miss something in your solution, acknowledge it honestly. Interviewers will appreciate your ability to recognize errors and fix them rather than pretending everything is perfect.
  - Example: "I realize now that I missed accounting for the possibility of empty inputs. Let me update my code to handle that case."

- **Ask for Help When Needed:** If you're struggling or feeling stuck, it's okay to ask for guidance. Interviewers often prefer candidates who are willing to seek help rather than waste time on a problem they can't solve.

- o Example: "I'm having some trouble with this part of the algorithm. Would you mind helping me clarify the next steps?"

3. Explaining Edge Cases and Assumptions:

- When you're testing your solution, explain the edge cases you've considered and any assumptions you've made. This helps the interviewer see that you are thinking about all potential scenarios and not just the typical case.
  - o Example: "I've handled the case where the input is an empty array, but I haven't yet considered the scenario where all elements are negative. Let me add that test case."

Non-Verbal Communication and How to Present Yourself Professionally

1. Posture and Body Language:

- **Sit Up Straight:** Maintain an open and engaged posture during the interview. Sitting up straight helps you appear confident and attentive.

- **Eye Contact:** Maintain **appropriate eye contact** with the interviewer to show that you are actively engaged and confident. However, don't overdo it to the point of discomfort.

- **Gestures:** Use natural hand gestures when explaining complex ideas, but be mindful not to overuse them. Gestures can make your explanation clearer and emphasize key points, but excessive movements can distract from your words.

2. Appearance and Attire:

- **Dress Professionally:** Your attire should reflect the company culture. In general, business casual is a safe choice for tech interviews, but if you're unsure, it's better to be slightly overdressed than underdressed.

  o For example, wearing a collared shirt or blouse with nice slacks or a modest dress shows that you are serious about the interview, while still fitting in with the casual nature of most tech companies.

- **Grooming:** Ensure that your grooming is neat and professional. Looking polished not only reflects well on you but also boosts your confidence.

3. Use of Technology (for Remote Interviews):

- **Check Your Setup:** For virtual interviews, ensure your internet connection is stable, your camera is positioned at eye level, and your microphone is clear. A poor technical setup can be distracting and take away from your performance.
- **Mute and Unmute:** If you're not speaking, make sure to **mute** your microphone to avoid background noise. When you're speaking, **unmute** promptly, and speak clearly into the mic.

4. Handling Nervousness:

- **Take a Deep Breath:** If you feel nervous, take a few deep breaths before starting. This can help calm your nerves and focus your mind.
- **Pace Yourself:** Don't rush through the problem-solving process. Take your time to think through the problem before diving into the solution. It's okay to pause and gather your thoughts.

Real-World Example: Demonstrating Effective Communication in an Interview

Scenario: Solving a LeetCode Problem – "Valid Parentheses"

Problem: Given a string containing just the characters '(', ')', '{', '}', '[', and ']', determine if the input string is valid. An input string is valid if:

- Open brackets must be closed by the same type of brackets.
- Open brackets must be closed in the correct order.

Step-by-Step Approach:

1. **Verbalizing the Problem:**
   - "We're given a string of parentheses, and we need to check if every opening parenthesis has a corresponding closing parenthesis in the correct order. To do this efficiently, I'll use a stack data structure because it's perfect for problems involving matching pairs and order."

2. **Outlining the Plan:**

o "I'll iterate through the string, and for every opening bracket, I'll push it onto the stack. For every closing bracket, I'll check if the stack contains a matching opening bracket at the top. If not, the string is invalid."

3. **Writing the Code:**

python

```python
def isValid(s):
    stack = []
    bracket_map = {')': '(', '}': '{', ']': '['}

    for char in s:
        if char in bracket_map:
            top_element = stack.pop() if stack else '#'
            if bracket_map[char] != top_element:
                return False
        else:
            stack.append(char)

    return not stack
```

4. **Testing and Explaining Edge Cases:**

- "Let me test this solution on a few cases. For example, s = "()", the output should be True because the parentheses are correctly paired. If s = "([)]", the output should be False because the order is incorrect."

- "Also, s = "" (an empty string) should return True because an empty string is trivially valid."

Conclusion

Effective **communication skills** and **interview etiquette** can make a huge difference in how you present yourself during a coding interview. By clearly articulating your thought process, maintaining transparency, and considering your **non-verbal communication**, you can demonstrate not only your technical abilities but also your ability to work well with others and navigate complex situations. Remember to stay calm, be clear, and present yourself confidently, and you'll be well on your way to performing successfully in interviews.

CHAPTER 26

PREPARING FOR SYSTEM DESIGN INTERVIEWS

System design interviews are an essential part of the interview process at many top tech companies. These interviews test your ability to design large-scale, distributed systems and evaluate your problem-solving skills, architecture knowledge, and ability to communicate complex ideas clearly. In this chapter, we'll explore what to expect in system design interviews, how to approach breaking down system design problems, how to effectively communicate your design choices, and real-world examples of system design solutions.

What to Expect in System Design Interviews and How to Prepare

1. Understanding the Purpose of System Design Interviews:

- System design interviews are designed to assess your ability to architect complex systems, considering performance, scalability, fault tolerance, and maintainability. You'll be asked to design a system that meets certain requirements, often involving scalability, high availability, and low latency.

- Unlike coding interviews, where you focus on algorithms and data structures, system design interviews require you to think about the system as a whole, breaking it into components, considering trade-offs, and addressing potential issues that could arise during development and deployment.

2. Common Topics Covered:

- **Scalability:** How to scale the system as the number of users grows.

- **Data Consistency:** Ensuring that data remains accurate and consistent across distributed systems.

- **High Availability and Fault Tolerance:** Designing systems that can continue to function even when parts of the system fail.

- **Caching:** Strategies for improving performance by storing frequently accessed data in memory.

- **Load Balancing:** Distributing traffic evenly across servers to avoid bottlenecks.
- **Database Design:** Choosing the right database system (SQL vs. NoSQL) and designing schemas for efficient data storage and retrieval.

3. How to Prepare:

- **Study System Design Fundamentals:** Familiarize yourself with key concepts in distributed systems, cloud computing, databases, and networking.
- **Practice Design Problems:** Work through common system design problems like designing a URL shortener, social media platform, or file storage system.
- **Review Existing Solutions:** Study the architecture of well-known systems (e.g., Google, Amazon, Facebook) to understand how large-scale systems are designed and why certain architectural choices are made.
- **Use Design Frameworks:** Learning structured frameworks like **Four-Step Approach (Define, Design, Scale, and Refine)** will help you approach system design systematically during interviews.

Approaches to Breaking Down System Design Problems

1. Clarify the Requirements:

- **Understand the Problem:** Begin by asking the interviewer clarifying questions to ensure that you understand the scope of the system. You need to be clear about the functional and non-functional requirements (e.g., scalability, latency, availability).
  - o Example Questions:
    - "What are the primary use cases for the system?"
    - "How much data will the system handle?"
    - "What is the expected traffic volume?"
    - "What is the acceptable latency for user interactions?"

2. Define System Constraints:

- Identify constraints that could impact your design. For example, budget constraints, time constraints, or technical limitations might affect your decisions.

    o   Example: "Are we allowed to use third-party services, or should the solution be entirely self-hosted?"

3. Break Down the Problem into Components:

- Divide the system into smaller, manageable components or services. For example, a messaging system could be divided into components like **user authentication**, **message storage**, **real-time message delivery**, and **notification services**.
- Each component should be designed to scale independently as needed.

4. Define APIs and Data Flow:

- Once you have a high-level understanding of the components, define how they will communicate with each other. This includes creating API definitions, message formats, and specifying data flow between services.
- For example, in a social media platform, the user service might expose APIs for creating a user, updating a user profile, and authenticating the user.

5. Identify Key Design Considerations:

- Think about scalability, availability, fault tolerance, and maintainability at each stage of the design. Consider the impact of each decision on performance and complexity.

- For example, should you use **sharding** for your database to handle large datasets? What type of **caching** solution will you implement to speed up frequently accessed data?

6. Evaluate Trade-Offs:

- As you design the system, evaluate the trade-offs between different architectural decisions. For example, if you're choosing between **SQL** and **NoSQL**, think about the pros and cons in terms of consistency, scalability, and flexibility.

How to Communicate Your Design Choices Effectively

1. Start with High-Level Overview:

- Begin by providing a high-level description of your design. Start with a block diagram to show how the various components interact with each other. This gives the interviewer a quick understanding of your approach.

- Example: "At a high level, our system consists of three main services: the User Service, the Message Service, and the Notification Service. The User Service handles authentication and profile management, the Message Service stores and delivers messages, and the Notification Service sends notifications to users."

2. Explain Each Component:

- Walk through each component in detail, explaining its responsibilities and how it interacts with other components. Be clear about the trade-offs behind each choice you make.
- Example: "For message storage, I'm using **NoSQL (Cassandra)** because it's designed to handle large amounts of data with high availability, which fits our need for horizontal scalability and distributed data."

3. Address Non-Functional Requirements:

- Discuss how your design meets non-functional requirements such as **scalability, availability, fault tolerance**, and **performance**.

  o Example: "To handle high traffic, I'm using **load balancing** to distribute requests across multiple servers. We will implement **caching** with **Redis** to reduce database load and improve response times."

4. Discuss Edge Cases and Trade-Offs:

- Address edge cases and how your system will handle them. Also, discuss trade-offs you made and why you chose one option over another.

  o Example: "In case of a sudden spike in traffic, we'll use **auto-scaling** to add more instances. However, this could introduce a delay in scaling up, so we'll need to monitor the system closely during high-demand periods."

5. Be Open to Feedback:

- After explaining your design, be prepared for the interviewer to ask questions or provide feedback.

They may challenge your design choices to test your reasoning and flexibility.

- o Example: "If the interviewer asks, 'What if the system needs to be even more fault-tolerant?', you could respond with, 'We could add **data replication** across multiple data centers to ensure higher availability, though this would increase complexity and cost.'"

Real-World Examples of System Design Solutions

1. Designing a URL Shortener (e.g., Bit.ly)

Problem: Design a system that takes long URLs and converts them into short, unique URLs.

High-Level Design:

- **Input:** Long URLs.
- **Output:** Short URLs that redirect to the original long URLs.
- **Components:**

- o **Frontend:** A simple web interface where users can input long URLs and get shortened URLs.
- o **Backend:** A service that stores the mapping of short URLs to long URLs.
- o **Database:** A database to store the long URLs and their corresponding short URLs.
- o **URL Generation:** A hash function or a sequential integer to generate the shortened URL.

Key Design Considerations:

- **Scalability:** Use **sharding** to distribute URLs across multiple databases as the system grows.
- **Availability:** Replicate data to ensure high availability.
- **Performance:** Cache frequently accessed URLs in **Redis** to reduce database load.

Example APIs:

- POST /shorten: Accepts a long URL and returns a short URL.

- GET /{short_url}: Redirects to the original long URL.

---

2. Designing a Social Media Platform (e.g., Facebook)

Problem: Design a system that allows users to post messages, comment, and like posts.

High-Level Design:

- **Frontend:** Web or mobile app where users can create posts, comment, and like posts.
- **Backend:** A set of services that manage users, posts, comments, likes, and notifications.
- **Database:** A relational database (e.g., **PostgreSQL**) for user data and a NoSQL database (e.g., **MongoDB**) for posts and comments.

Key Design Considerations:

- **Scalability:** Use **sharding** for user data and post data to handle large amounts of content.

- **High Availability:** Use **replication** and **load balancing** to ensure that the service remains available during high traffic periods.

- **Fault Tolerance:** Implement **caching** (e.g., **Redis**) for popular posts to improve response time and reduce database load.

Example APIs:

- POST /users: Creates a new user account.
- POST /posts: Allows users to create posts.
- GET /posts/{user_id}: Retrieves a user's posts.
- POST /likes: Allows users to like a post.
- POST /comments: Allows users to comment on a post.

Conclusion

Preparing for **system design interviews** requires understanding how to break down complex problems, communicate your design choices clearly, and consider key non-functional requirements such as scalability, performance, and fault tolerance. By practicing with real-world examples and learning to present your solutions systematically, you will build the skills needed to succeed in these interviews. Whether designing a URL shortener or a social media platform, the principles of good system design—clear communication, modular components, and scalability—will help guide your approach and make you a strong candidate.

CHAPTER 27

FINAL TIPS FOR ACING YOUR TECH INTERVIEW

The journey to acing a **tech interview** can be challenging, but with the right preparation and mindset, you can maximize your chances of success. In this chapter, we will recap the strategies for excelling in both **coding** and **system design interviews**, offer tips for staying positive and focused throughout the process, provide additional resources for continued learning, and discuss how to make a lasting impression to stand out as a candidate.

Recap of Strategies for Acing Coding and System Design Interviews

1. Preparing for Coding Interviews:

- **Master Core Algorithms and Data Structures:** Focus on the foundational algorithms and data structures (e.g., arrays, linked lists, trees, dynamic programming, and graphs). Practice common

305

problem types across platforms like **LeetCode**, **HackerRank**, and **CodeSignal**.

- **Solve Problems Actively:** Don't just passively read solutions. Actively solve coding problems, verbalize your thought process, and work through edge cases.

- **Time Yourself:** Practice solving problems within time constraints to simulate real interview conditions. Use platforms that provide timed challenges or set your own time limits.

- **Review and Refactor:** After solving a problem, review your solution for efficiency, clarity, and simplicity. Consider how you can optimize the code in terms of time and space complexity.

2. Preparing for System Design Interviews:

- **Learn Key Concepts:** Study distributed systems, load balancing, database design, and scalability. Understand the trade-offs between different architectures (e.g., NoSQL vs. SQL, monolithic vs. microservices).

- **Practice with Real-World Problems:** Use real-world system design problems to simulate interviews. Examples include designing a URL shortener, a social media platform, or a file storage system.

- **Use Structured Approaches:** Follow structured approaches like **Four-Step Design (Define, Design, Scale, Refine)** to break down system design problems. Always start with clarifying requirements, then design components, address non-functional requirements, and refine your solution with feedback.

- **Communicate Clearly:** Practice explaining your design decisions step-by-step, discussing trade-offs, and answering follow-up questions from the interviewer.

3. Behavioral Interview Preparation:

- **Understand Common Behavioral Questions:** Prepare answers for common questions like "Tell me about a time when you worked in a team," "How do you handle failure?" and "Describe a challenging problem you solved."

- **Use the STAR Method:** Structure your answers using the STAR method (Situation, Task, Action, Result) to provide clear, concise, and complete responses.

- **Showcase Your Soft Skills:** Highlight your ability to work in teams, communicate effectively, and manage stress. Be honest about mistakes, and show how you learn from challenges.

How to Stay Positive and Focused Throughout the Interview Process

1. Mental Preparation:

- **Visualize Success:** Visualizing success can help calm your nerves and reduce anxiety. Before the interview, take a moment to close your eyes, breathe deeply, and imagine yourself succeeding.
- **Stay Positive:** Interviews are stressful, but maintaining a positive attitude will help you remain focused and perform better. If you encounter a difficult question, stay calm and view it as an opportunity to showcase your problem-solving skills.
- **Embrace the Learning Process:** Even if you don't get the job, consider the interview as an opportunity to learn. Reflect on the experience and identify areas where you can improve for the next round.

2. Managing Stress:

- **Practice Deep Breathing:** If you feel anxious, take slow, deep breaths to help relax your body and mind. Deep breathing exercises can calm your nerves and allow you to think more clearly during the interview.
- **Take Short Pauses:** During coding or system design interviews, don't hesitate to take a brief moment to collect your thoughts. It's better to pause, think, and solve the problem methodically than to rush through it.

3. Focus on the Process, Not Just the Outcome:

- Remember that interviews are a two-way process. While the company is evaluating your skills, you are also assessing if the company and role are a good fit for you. Stay focused on demonstrating your skills and enjoy the challenge.

Additional Resources for Continued Learning and Improvement

1. Online Coding Platforms:

- **LeetCode:** Offers a vast collection of coding problems, including interview-style challenges and mock interview questions.

- **HackerRank:** Provides coding challenges and competitions with a focus on algorithms, data structures, and interview prep.

- **CodeSignal:** Offers practice tests and assessments used by companies for hiring, along with personal challenges to hone your skills.

- **Exercism:** Focuses on exercises and mentorship to improve your coding in various programming languages.

2. System Design Resources:

- **Grokking the System Design Interview (Educative):** A great resource for mastering system design interviews with in-depth lessons and examples.

- **Designing Data-Intensive Applications by Martin Kleppmann:** A deep dive into the concepts of scalability, databases, and distributed systems.

- **YouTube Channels (e.g., Gaurav Sen, System Design Interview):** Various tech YouTubers explain complex system design concepts with real-world examples.

3. Books and Articles:

- **Cracking the Coding Interview by Gayle Laakmann McDowell:** A comprehensive guide to preparing for coding interviews, including detailed practice problems and solutions.
- **Elements of Programming Interviews by Adnan Aziz:** A highly recommended book for interview prep, with hundreds of problems and solutions.
- **The System Design Interview by Alex Xu:** A great resource that focuses specifically on preparing for system design interviews with real-world examples and structured approaches.

How to Make the Best Impression and Stand Out as a Candidate

1. Be Confident, but Humble:

- Confidence is essential in interviews, but humility is equally important. While you should present your skills and experience confidently, acknowledge that you're always open to learning and improving.

- **Example:** "I've worked with databases extensively, but I'd be eager to dive deeper into distributed databases if given the opportunity at your company."

2. Show Enthusiasm and Interest:

- Express your excitement about the company and role. Research the company's mission, products, and culture to demonstrate your genuine interest.
- **Example:** "I'm really excited about the opportunity to work with your team, especially because of your company's focus on scalability and innovative product development. I believe my experience with cloud architectures aligns well with your needs."

3. Ask Thoughtful Questions:

- Asking insightful questions shows that you are genuinely interested in the company and the role. These questions can focus on the team structure, technology stack, or growth opportunities.

- **Example:** "What is the team culture like at your company? How do you approach ongoing learning and professional development for engineers?"

4. Be Clear and Concise:

- When communicating your ideas, avoid rambling. Be concise, but thorough in your explanations. Focus on the core aspects of your design, solution, or experience without overcomplicating things.
- **Example:** "My approach to solving this problem is using a hash map to store frequencies, which will give us an efficient $O(n)$ time complexity. Here's how the code would look..."

5. Demonstrate Teamwork and Collaboration:

- Tech companies value collaboration and the ability to work effectively with cross-functional teams. Highlight examples of how you've worked in teams and communicated across disciplines.
- **Example:** "In my previous role, I worked closely with product managers and designers to ensure that the solutions we developed met both technical and user experience requirements."

Conclusion

Acing a **tech interview** involves more than just technical proficiency. It requires a combination of strong problem-solving skills, effective communication, and professionalism. By following the strategies discussed in this chapter—preparing thoroughly for coding and system design interviews, maintaining a positive and calm demeanor, using available resources for continued learning, and making a strong impression during the interview—you can position yourself for success.

Remember that the interview is an opportunity to showcase your abilities and demonstrate your fit for the role. With the right preparation, mindset, and approach, you'll be ready to tackle any interview challenge and stand out as a top candidate. Good luck!

* 9 7 9 8 3 1 5 5 3 5 7 5 1 *